Praise for Leaves, Roots & Fruit

"Required reading before any tomato plants are sold to anyone anywhere. Nicole taught me this concept years ago and I've never forgotten it."
— **Myquillyn Smith**, *New York Times* best-selling author of *Welcome Home*

"Nicole inspires us all to dive deeper into sustainability with her beautiful and functional kitchen garden process, full of details that could give anyone a strong foundation to become a lifelong gardener."
— **Jen Hansard**, best-selling author of *Simple Green Smoothies* and *Simple Green Meals*

"*Leaves, Roots & Fruit* simplifies the process of learning to garden in an easy-to-use format, and the photos are gorgeous. Highly recommend!"
— **Lauren Liess**, author of *Feels Like Home*, *Down to Earth*, and *Habitat*

"The perfect book to help you add the habit of gardening into your everyday life— even if you've never thought to call yourself a 'gardener.'"
— **Jessica Honegger**, author of *Imperfect Courage* and host of the *Going Scared* podcast

"A relevant and relatable must-have for gardeners of all experience levels. Nicole serves as a knowledgeable yet engaging coach as she walks you through the ins and outs of how to create a personalized gardening system that works for YOU!"
— **Ashlie Thomas**, the Mocha Gardener and author of *How to Become a Gardener*

"Nicole has demystified the process of basic backyard, small-scale gardening for food or flowers into a simple and easy-to-follow step system. She will take you by the hand and walk you through the steps in word and image, physically and intellectually, for you to beautifully and deliciously grow into the kitchen gardener you want to be!"
— **Jennifer Jewell**, creator and host of the award-winning public radio program and podcast *Cultivating Place*

"Gardeners of all levels—from the first-time small-space gardener to a gardener like me with experience and space—will find more success in their gardens after getting their hands on this book and implementing this easy-to-understand system."
— **Jill McSheehy**, host of the *Beginner's Garden* podcast and author of *Vegetable Gardening for Beginners*

Leaves,
Roots
& Fruit

Also by Nicole Johnsey Burke

*Kitchen Garden Revival: A Modern Guide to Creating a Stylish
Small-Scale, Low-Maintenance Edible Garden*

Leaves, Roots & Fruit

A STEP-BY-STEP GUIDE TO PLANTING AN ORGANIC KITCHEN GARDEN

Nicole Johnsey Burke
PHOTOGRAPHY BY Eric Kelley

HAY HOUSE, INC.

Carlsbad, California • New York City
London • Sydney • New Delhi

Published in the United States by: Hay House, Inc.: www.hayhouse.com® •
Published in Australia by: Hay House Australia Pty. Ltd.: www.hayhouse.com.
au • Published in the United Kingdom by: Hay House UK, Ltd.: www
.hayhouse.co.uk • Published in India by: Hay House Publishers India: www
.hayhouse.co.in

Indexer: Joan D. Shapiro
Cover and interior design: Karla Schweer
Interior photos: Eric Kelley

Cataloging-in-Publication Data is on file at the Library of Congress

Hardcover ISBN: 978-1-4019-6910-3
E-book ISBN: 978-1-4019-6911-0
Audiobook ISBN: 978-1-4019-6912-7

10 9 8 7 6 5 4 3 2 1
1st edition, December 2022

Printed in China

dedication

FOR MY PARENTS, Dennis and Klydell, who taught me to never stop growing and always gave me just what I needed to take the next step.

CONTENTS

preface

A new garden system

If you've put off gardening or quit gardening or not even tried gardening because you thought you didn't have enough: enough space, enough sun, enough time, enough experience, or enough patience, this book is for you.

These words, photos, and steps are for anyone who's not gardening because they don't yet "have enough." What you're about to read isn't just a how-to book on gardening; it's a gardening system that matches what you already have with a plant that needs exactly what you've got. This eight-step system follows the order of plant growth and shows you that no matter how little or how much space, time, sun, or experience you have in any given season, there's always a plant you can grow right where you are, right away.

There's something in these pages for every level of gardening skill—whether you're just starting out or you've been growing for a few seasons. The Leaves, Roots, and Fruit (LRF) system and these stories developed out of my own mistake-ridden gardening journey and my work helping thousands of gardeners—most claiming they had no "green thumb"—start filling our own harvest baskets even when we didn't quite have "enough." If we've found a way to grow something beautiful and delicious out of what we already have, I know you can too.

Keep up with your garden progress and find more support to grow with the Leaves, Roots & Fruit journal, available as a free download at leavesrootsandfruit.com.

part one

the leaves, roots & fruit system

"We need a garden," I said to my husband, Jason, on the way home from visiting my parents, where my mom's cherry tomato vines were thick with sweet red fruit that our kids picked by the handful and ate straight off the plant. Before he said a word, I already had visions of strolling in from the backyard, my harvest basket full of homegrown food we would eat for dinner each night.

My dreams had no patience. So as soon as I got home, we did what most people do when they're starting a garden—we drove straight to the home-improvement store. We selected the largest, most promising tomato plants and proudly strapped them into the back seat of our minivan.

There were only 99 things wrong with what we did here, but I'll start with 3:

One, we began with the tomato, one of the most demanding vegetables (technically, it's a fruit, but we'll discuss that later).

Two, we bought plants before we'd even begun to set up the garden space.

Three, we planted in the middle of July, paying no attention to seasons or the time of year that tomato plants prefer.

Fast-forward two months, and I didn't need a harvest basket to carry the three

tomatoes the raccoons hadn't eaten as I came in from a garden full of weeds.

Unfazed by our lack of success in year one, we planted tomatoes again a second summer, this time in small raised beds. We also attempted cucumbers in a pot on the deck and crossed our fingers when we planted a few watermelon seeds too. Though our garden setup was a little better and our timing improved, we rarely beat the raccoons to the tomatoes, we watched the cucumbers dry up by midsummer, and we never saw a single watermelon.

That second failed attempt nearly convinced me that gardening wasn't going to work for me. *Gardening must be for people who grew up on a farm, who worked with plants their whole life*, I thought. People who had way more time on their hands. People who had that thing called a "green thumb."

After two rounds of disappointment, it was clear that we couldn't keep doing what we had been doing and expect success. We needed a do-over.

The next year, instead of digging into the lawn to plant our veggies, we built taller raised beds and ordered a truckload of the best soil we could get. Instead of heading to the store for plants, we toured our friends' garden and accepted some of their extra seed packets, with names like 'Rocky Top' lettuce, dwarf Siberian kale, wild rocket arugula, purple mustard—so many plants I'd never even thought about having in a garden.

Once the raised beds were set and filled with soil, we opened the seed packets and went for it.

And in just a few months, we harvested a million times more than we did from our first two gardens combined. (I may be exaggerating here, but not by much.)

For the next six months, we were picking something every day, enjoying salads, smoothies, and delicious, garden-fresh dishes—and sharing armloads of harvests with friends and neighbors.

It took three seasons and a lot of dead plants for my garden-to-table vision to come true. But when I was skipping past big sections of the produce aisle (because all those foods were growing in my kitchen garden), it was official: I was definitely a "gardener" now.

And there wasn't a single tomato in sight.

The Eight Steps to Success

My own garden journey taught me the hard way what I'll share inside this book: You don't need to be a "pro" or possess a green thumb to become a gardener. You don't even need a "certain amount" of something to begin. Once you have a garden system, growing a little (or a lot) of your own organic, delicious food can be part of your everyday life, any day of the year.

That first summer, if I'd looked more closely at my mom's garden, I

would've noticed that her space was mostly green—full of leaves, with hints of colorful fruit here and there. I would've seen that those sweet tomatoes were growing on vines that had been planted months earlier. A more thorough look would've shown me that beneath that tall vine of tomatoes were plants growing at every level below: bushes of basil, arugula leaves, garlic, and green onions too.

And the secret to success in the garden, I ultimately realized, was to follow the vine down to ground level and start there: first with leaves, then with roots, and finally with fruiting plants.

Let me explain . . .

Pretend there's a staircase between you and the ability to grow just about anything in your own garden. You're standing at the bottom, and your biggest harvest goals are waiting at the top. Imagine there are eight steps on this staircase, and each step represents a plant's increasing need for sunlight, space, time, and attention. The lower the step, the less the plants need—from you and nature—to thrive. The higher up the staircase, the more resources and care the plants require.

You following me?

This set of steps is a gardening system. You can start your garden journey at the first level and, with each step, learn how to grow a new set of delicious and nutritious plants that you harvest and eat during your climb to the top.

Your first step won't require a lot—not a lot of sunlight, not a lot of time, and not a lot of space. In fact, it's possible to begin inside on your windowsill.

With each step you climb, you'll need more light, more space, and more time (time for your plants to grow and time you commit to caring for these plants). The plants on Step 1 are small and manageable inside your home, but by Step 7, they're sprawling, large enough to create a maze for you to walk through.

You might be tempted to take a flying leap straight up to Step 6 (that's where the tomatoes grow), but trust me: it's more fun (and less frustrating) to go one step at a time.

Grow with Your Plants

"Ask not what your plant can do for you, but what you can do for your plant."

I didn't get the quote exactly right, but the point is that having empathy makes learning to garden so much simpler. Though it's tempting to focus only on the harvest basket, it's actually more productive to think less about what we as gardeners want and more about what our plants require to flourish—in other words, "plant motives." If we can learn what motivates plants to grow, and if we garden with those goals in mind, keeping plants alive becomes less of a mystery.

I became aware of plant motives when my children were little. I was constantly looking for activities that were fun and noncompetitive and didn't result in a huge mess in the living room. This translated into a lot of hikes and time at the park. And on one fall afternoon, our walk brought us along a path of giant oak trees.

After just a few steps, my littlest, new to walking, fell. Oops! When she stood and brushed herself off, we realized she'd tripped over a huge pile of acorns.

To keep her from crying, we made a game of counting the acorns around our feet. "One, two, three . . ." We lost count somewhere around 398.

This acorn incident happened right after my first "failed" garden, and counting all those seeds on the ground piqued my disappointed gardener's interest.

Why on earth, I wondered, would this one tree drop thousands, if not millions, of acorns right below its own branches every year?

I'm no botanist, but at least one answer seemed clear: that oak tree was hedging its bets. It was doing everything it could to keep its species alive. Not just alive, but thriving, spreading, multiplying.

Those oak trees helped me start thinking about what makes plants tick, or rather, keep on growing. I didn't have all the answers, but if the acorns were any indication, it was becoming clear that plants are mainly motivated to survive and to make more plants.

And I was thinking that this was very good news.

Any time you feel confused in the garden, think about this first: plants are

Four Things about Plants

What makes a plant a plant and not something else? There are (at least) four things:

Plants feed themselves. And we're complaining that it's difficult to be a gardener? Puppies, kittens, toddlers, even goldfish need us to feed them every day. But no matter how many plants you're growing, you can rest assured that if placed in the right spot, each one can gather its own food supply quite well on its own, thank you very much.

Plants don't have feet. It's a good thing plants can feed themselves because they can't get up and walk to the fridge. Plants stay planted. It's this fact that makes choosing a location for your plants so important.

Plants are tough. Plant cells can be hit with rain and wind—and, for some plants, even hail and snow—and still not break. "Tough as nails?" "Tough as plants" sounds more like it.

Plants can grow forever. Under certain conditions, plants never stop growing. Along stems and roots is a type of plant tissue with cells that multiply again and again, so those stems and roots continuously grow longer and wider. They can't stop, won't stop unless a storm or a hard freeze or a gardener (ahem) steps in.

Put these four things together and you realize plants are exceptionally smart. The plants you'll grow on each step in your gardening journey know how to grow themselves. They know what to do every step of the way. Now you just need to make it suitable for them to do their thing.

dying to survive. They need (and want) to live through all their stages of life, and they don't want to die before they've created hundreds, if not thousands, more plants just like themselves.

Aha moments like these help us realize that gardening is less of a power struggle and more like a partnership. By focusing on what plants want to do, you'll know what matters most to the plants you're hoping to grow. When you view gardening as working *alongside* plants, helping them do the things they're naturally motivated to do, the process of gardening becomes simpler—even if you do find yourself falling down every now and again.

The Leaves, Roots, and Fruit system guides you to grow with your plants, focusing at first on plants with harvests that are ready quickly and without much tending, and then graduating to plants that need more time and space before harvest as your experience in the garden grows.

Grow with your plants. LRF follows the growth cycle of plants, catching certain plants at each level of their growth so that you get to enjoy the success of quick growth and impressive harvests within days of planting your first seed. As you plant more and harvest more with some of the simplest plants, you'll build the experience necessary to be ready to grow plants that need more time and attention. And step by step, you'll eventually learn how to grow just about anything in the kitchen garden—not because of luck or a green thumb, but because you now understand how plants grow.

To grow with our plant, we first need to know *how* our plants grow.

Seeds, roots, sprouts, stems, leaves, flowers, fruit, seeds.

That's the full growth cycle of most kitchen garden plants. Some plants skip the fruiting stage, but almost all plants eventually produce some type of flower to house some type of seed. And every plant, of course, produces leaves—lots of them. Once you know all the pieces of the growth puzzle, you'll start to understand how the garden system works.

Seeds

We start with the seed. A seed is the reproductive part of the plant that is ready for growth. Most seeds have three structures: a seed coat for protection, an embryo (complete with roots, stems, and leaves inside) that will turn into the new plant once the seed germinates, and a food store (called the endosperm) to feed the baby plant until it can produce its own food through photosynthesis.

To transition from seed to seedling, a seed needs three things: water, oxygen, and warmth. First, the seed's tough outer coating absorbs nearby H_2O and oxygen and begins to swell. The cells inside the seed embryo enlarge. Then warmth from the soil gives more energy to the cells

within the seed, speeding up the cell replication process.

Finally, the embryo becomes so swollen that the seed coat breaks open and the first root, known as the radicle, emerges into the soil. The endosperm provides a quick food source for the embryo, and germination is now considered complete. The seed has moved into the next stage of growth.

Roots and Sprouts

Once the primary root escapes the seed coating, the seed is officially a sprout. As this first root makes its way into the soil, it gathers new supplies for the sprouting plant: more water, more nutrients, more air.

Next up comes the mesocotyl, the first part of the stem. Instead of growing down like the radicle, the mesocotyl

reaches through the crown of the seed, up and up and up in search of light, until it breaks the soil surface.

Attached to the mesocotyl are the cotyledons, a set of two "false leaves" or seed leaves—so called because they are simple and do not look like the plant's adult foliage. The cotyledons are the first leaves to absorb the rays of sunlight and bring a new source of energy to the tiny plant, powering it to head into the next stage of growth.

Stems

The initial stem is the second part of the plant to appear above the soil line after the cotyledon breaks the soil's surface. The stem produces new cells at its tip to grow the first set of "true leaves"—those that look and function like the leaves the plant will produce for the rest of its life.

Stems are the support structure for all the leaves, flowers, and fruit that will come during the plant's life cycle. Its cell walls are the toughest of all the cells in the plant. Because stems provide the highway for food dispersal and reproduction, they have built-in protectors that mean not only better success for the plant in the wild but also more success in your garden.

Leaves

Leaves are the outgrowths of the plant that are connected directly to the stem. They are the workers of the plant, gathering energy from the sun, taking in air, and soaking up water from the atmosphere and the stem to make food and energy for the plant all day long. Remember? Plants feed themselves.

Each new leaf is both a factory and a warehouse. Leaves use chlorophyll to turn sunlight into plant food, and they're the most necessary part of the plant for its continued growth. Sure, roots provide stability and nutrient uptake, stems are important for support and structure, and flowers are critical for reproduction. But without leaves, there would be no more stem or root or flower or fruit, because there would be no energy to power growth.

Flowers

After stems and leaves come flowers. And flowers are all about survival. (Plant motives matter.)

In a plant's life cycle, flowers appear after the stems and leaves reach a certain point of maturity or when the plant senses that conditions are changing and it needs to speed up its reproductive cycle.

Flowers contain the reproductive organs necessary for a plant to create many more of its own kind. While wild animals hedge their bets by bearing several offspring in each litter, flowers are next-level, creating hundreds if not thousands of times more chances at continuing their kind.

Most flowers include both male and female parts and may or may not require the aid of an insect, animal, or other outside influence for pollination. When a creature is necessary for pollination, the flower almost always has a way to attract it—perhaps multiple petals that serve as a landing pad, a long throat to encourage nectar sipping, or a fragrance. Plants may not be able to speak, but they're certainly not silent. They have their own ways of getting assistance to make reproductive magic happen.

Fruit

Assuming the flower is pollinated by bee or butterfly or wind, the plant enters one of its final stages, setting fruit. In most cases, each flower represents one fruit, and the fruit often forms right inside the flower itself.

Fruit consists of an outer coating, an inner layer of tissue, and, oftentimes, lots and lots of seeds. Fruit typically takes as long to ripen as it does to form, so the larger the fruit, the more days you will need not only for the fruit to grow to its full size but also for it to fully ripen and sweeten.

To the plant, fruit is its promise that its species will keep growing for seasons and years to come. When you bite into that tomato or slice open the cucumber, you'll see why. Hidden inside that protective skin and juicy pulp are dozens, if not hundreds, of seeds. The fruit not only protects the precious seeds but also ensures the seeds will be transported—by animal or human—to places where the mama plant can't go, where it can then grow into another plant, same but different, in the next season. Plants don't have feet, but they still know how to travel.

Seeds

Plants end their life cycles as they began: with seeds.

After a flower turns to fruit and that fruit hangs on the vine, bush, or tree, one of a few things will happen. Left on its own, the fruit will slowly crack open, wilt, or dry up, and the seeds will either remain inside the dry pod or fall to the ground along with the spoiled pulp. If the fruit happens to catch the eye of a hungry animal or human passing by, that fruit will get eaten, and perhaps the seeds will be discarded or passed along in a (well-fertilized) way.

Most seeds need to dry and go through a dormant stage before they can sprout and start again. They need a break (a month or even a full calendar year) before they can begin the process all over again.

But don't let their sleepy appearance fool you. Hidden inside that pebble-like seed is the promise of many future harvests and a clear plan to do it all again next season. Give this seed a rest, and soon it will burrow down into the dark earth; swell with water and warmth; and burst open to reveal the start of another plant that will, with the right conditions, repeat this process again and again and again.

Set Up for Success

"My house was known as 'the place where the dead fern grows.'"

She and her daughter laughed and said these words to me as we walked through her kitchen garden together, picking cherry tomatoes, squash, eggplants, and arugula. There weren't any ferns to speak of, but nothing looked dead here.

I met Anu when she moved into her new home and wanted a kitchen garden as a centerpiece. Now, a few years later, she was stepping out each day to harvest something for dinner. This former "plant killer" was living "garden to table" using fresh greens and harvests from her own garden each week in the family meals.

So what changed?

Her setup.

Instead of growing a few plants here and there or trying to water a few pots on the front porch, Anu now had a dedicated space for the garden created with tall and wide raised beds that were easy to access and perfect for deep-rooted plants. The location was chosen to maximize the sunlight her plants could receive each day of the year. The soil was prepared using local compost that was replenished every season before being planted again. The plants and seeds were spaced just right. Watering was automated and consistent, thanks to drip lines installed throughout each bed. The time required in the garden? Less than half an hour of tending and harvesting each day.

With each step you take in the garden, take a note from Anu to ensure your yard doesn't become "the place where the dead fern grows." Take the time to set up your garden to incorporate the necessary inputs for each step from the beginning. Sunlight, space, time and temperature, water, nutrients, and care: these are the key inputs no matter what you're growing in the Leaves, Roots, and Fruit system. And light is of first importance.

Sunlight

Consider sunlight as the energy source for your garden plants. The rays from the sun hit your plants' leaves and literally "turn them on."

All plants need sunlight to grow, but some need more than others. When leaves absorb enough sunlight, they use the sun's energy to break down water molecules (brought into the plant

through its roots) and carbon dioxide molecules (which enter the plant through tiny holes in its leaves, flowers, stems, and roots) into glucose (sugar) and oxygen. This sugar circulates through the plant to provide energy for new growth or cell repair, and the oxygen is released back into the atmosphere.

This is the magical process known as photosynthesis.

The rate at which leaves can photosynthesize depends on the amount of light that reaches the leaves, the ambient temperature, and the availability of water and nutrients like nitrogen and phosphorus.

In other words, your plant's growing time is directly tied to its sunning time.

But just because your plants need light to grow doesn't mean your plants' leaves have to bathe in direct sunlight from sunrise to sunset. In fact, each plant's light needs are different, depending on species, growth habit, and reproductive cycle.

Setup for the Leaves, Roots, and Fruit System

	STEP 1: SPROUTS AND MICROGREENS	STEP 2: HERBS	STEP 3: SALAD GREENS	STEP 4: ROOTS
CONTAINER	Seed-starting tray 4–6 inches deep	Container or raised bed 12 inches tall	Container or raised bed 6–12 inches tall	Raised bed 6–12 inches tall
PLANT SPACING	Seeds are scattered but not overlapping	1–6 per square foot	1–16 per square foot	6–36 per square foot
SOIL	Seed-starting mix	Sandy loam soil	Compost and topsoil mix	103 mix (see page 69)
SUNLIGHT	0 hours for sprouts; 10–12 hours of artificial light for microgreens	2–4 hours per day	4–6 hours per day	6–8 hours per day
TEMPERATURE	45–75°F	45–75°F+	45–65°F	45–75°F
WATER	Rinse sprouts daily; add 1 inch of water to bottom tray for microgreens	1 inch of water per week or when soil is dry	Check moisture level daily; never let soil dry completely	1 inch of water per week
TIME	5–7 days for sprouts; 10–21 days for microgreens	25–60 days	30–60 days	35–90+ days

STEP 5: TUBERS, BULBS, AND RHIZOMES	STEP 6: SMALL FRUIT	STEP 7: LARGE FRUIT	STEP 8: SEEDS
Raised bed 12 inches tall	Raised bed 18 inches tall	Raised bed 18 inches tall or row garden	Row garden
6 per square foot to 1 per 2 square feet	1 per 1–3 square feet	1 per 1–3 square feet	4–6 per square foot
103 mix (see page 69)	103 mix (see page 69)	Compost-amended topsoil	Compost-amended topsoil
6–8 hours per day	8–12 hours per day	10–12 hours per day	10+ hours per day
45–75°F+ (90°F+ for ginger and sweet potatoes)	65–85°F	65–85°F	75°F+
1 inch of water per week	1 inch of water per week	1 inch of water per week per square foot of plant growth	1–2 inches of water per week
30–90+ days	75–90 days	90–120+ days	100+ days

As you learn the LRF system, you'll better understand the light needs of the particular plant you're aiming to grow. But when in doubt, think about the stages of plant growth. If you're growing a plant to harvest in its earlier stage of growth—leaf or stem—then that plant will need less hours of light. Similarly, if you're hoping to harvest a plant at a later stage—fruit or seed—then more hours of light each day is necessary.

No matter their sunlight needs, most plants will survive in less than optimal light for their species; they just won't thrive. If you're okay with plants taking longer to mature or growing but not maturing fully, you can have more flexibility when it comes to your garden's sunlight needs.

If you plan to grow in a container or a raised bed but haven't set up the site yet, find a spot that gets as much

SUNLIGHT NEEDS PER STEP

	STEPS 1 & 2: SPROUTS AND HERBS	STEP 3: LEAFY GREENS	STEPS 4 & 5: ROOTS, BULBS, AND TUBERS	STEPS 6 & 7: SMALL AND LARGE FRUIT	STEP 8: SEEDS
DAILY HOURS OF SUNLIGHT	2–4	4–6	6–8	8–10+	10+

sunlight as possible. Light should be your number one priority when selecting a location for your raised beds. In the Northern Hemisphere, place your garden on the south side of any tall structures like fences, homes, or trees so it will still receive winter sunlight (on the northern side if you're in the Southern Hemisphere).

After you've selected locations that maximize sunlight, you can narrow down your decision on where to place the containers or beds based on proximity to a water source, easy access to the kitchen, and overall aesthetics in the landscape.

Space

Just like with light and time, the space in which your plants are allowed to grow is directly correlated to their production. For an 8- to 10-pound harvest of cucumbers, your cucumber vines will need to grow 8 to 10 feet long. But you can grow 1 pound of radishes in less than 1 square foot.

In fact, with a few exceptions, the heavier and larger the harvest in pounds, the more space in square feet is required. A small bowl of sprouts will grow in less than a square foot. Growing a large, ripe sphere of melon will require at least 10 times that amount of room. Each leaf or root or fruit crop grown requires an entire plant system to support it, so the larger the harvest, the larger the growing space required.

As you progress from one LRF step to the next, you'll increase your growing space a little at a time. Have only a windowsill to grow on? No worries. Got an entire backyard to fill? We can do that too. Here's a preview of the amount of gardening space we fill at each step in this book.

STEP 1: ½ to 1 square foot

STEP 2: ½ to 1 square foot

STEP 3: 1 square foot

STEP 4: 1 square foot

STEP 5: 1 to 2 square feet

STEP 6: 2 to 3 square feet

STEP 7: 3 to 10 square feet

STEP 8: 1 to 10 square feet

For Steps 1 through 3, set up a container space.

When looking for a container for your herbs or salad greens, keep in mind each plant's potential growth, not just the size it is now. A pot that's too small for a growing plant means the plant can't send its roots deeper to reach for more nutrients or water when it needs it. You'll have greater success picking a pot that's at least as deep and wide, as the plant will grow up and out.

Instead of growing each plant in its own pot, try planting all of your herbs or salad greens in one large container together. Look for a container that's about 4 feet wide and at least 8 to 12 inches deep to give each plant enough room to stretch out its roots.

Choose a natural or food-safe material for your pot or container, such as terra-cotta, stainless steel, or natural fiber bag. Look for words like *food grade* and *untreated* so you don't have to worry about anything unsafe leaching into your food. If the container you select doesn't have holes, drill your own to ensure proper drainage so plants' roots don't sit in water and rot.

For Steps 4 through 6 or 7, set up a raised-bed space.

Raised beds provide the ideal growing conditions for many fruiting plants and vegetables with roots that like to dig down deep. In addition to keeping your garden looking attractive, raised beds allow you to start with the best soil possible, maintain more consistent soil temperature, and provide better drainage—not to mention that tending a raised-bed garden is so much easier.

When selecting materials for your raised beds, choose a natural material. For wood, there's untreated cedar, redwood, or hemlock. Stone, corten steel, and powder-coated steel also make beautiful and durable raised-bed containers.

For Steps 6 and 8, use supports and trellises for your space in a raised-bed garden or row garden.

Trellises offer needed support and maximize growing space by giving climbing plants a place to grow up instead of out. By holding plants in place, trellises help maintain good airflow and make tending easier, keeping both your vining plants and their neighbors healthy. The best trellises allow plants to grow on the outside of the support structure. Panel, obelisk, and arch trellises double your growing space as vines grow up, not just out.

Time and Temperature

After light and space, time and temperature are the critical factors when considering what to plant and when to plant it. Each plant has its own speed by which it moves through its stages of sprout, root, stem, leaf, flower, fruit, and seed.

In its DNA, each plant has an internal clock, a sense of how long it needs to rest, how long it needs to go from seed to seedling at a certain temperature,

Good Things Take Time

It can be tempting to buy synthetic fertilizer with the intent to speed up your plants' production, but the reality is that plants are genetically programmed to need a certain amount of sunlight and a certain amount of darkness at particular temperature ranges to reach full maturity. While you can do some things to raise or drop the temperature, no "miracle" can make the sun rise and set faster. Just remember, good things take time.

and how long it takes to grow big enough to produce a whole lot of new seeds, assuming it's exposed to the right amounts of sunlight, temperature, and moisture. Instead of cycling from 12 to 12, this plant clock goes from seed to seed, and a lot of that timing is dependent on air and soil temperature.

Before you plant a seed, it's important to remember what part of the plant you plan to harvest—the leaves, roots, or fruit—and how much time that plant needs to germinate from seed and reach that stage. Read the backs of seed packets and you'll learn that different plants require different amounts of time to develop within a given temperature range.

Check your calendar. Do you have enough time in the gardening season for the plant to mature to the desired stage before the temperatures or seasons shift? Leaves need a number of days, roots need weeks, and fruit needs months, sometimes years.

In general, most cool-season plants will wait until soil temperatures are above 40°F to start growing, whereas most warm-season plants wait for the soil to surpass 55°F or even 65°F. Once growth begins, most cool-season plants have an internal thermometer that will begin seed production as soon as temperatures go above 75 or 80°F; warm-season plants do the same around 90°F.

This minimum and maximum temperature means that each plant you grow has a unique "on/off" switch that's more in charge of the plant than you are, which also means a lot of the times you thought you were the one to blame for your plant's failure, it was really the switch that was in charge.

As you progress through this garden system, you'll learn how to pay attention to the timing, how to anticipate how many days your plant needs to reach the point you're hoping to harvest, and how to make the most of the days you have even if the timing isn't perfect.

TIME AND TEMPERATURE REQUIREMENTS BY PLANT STAGE

STAGE	TIME	TEMPERATURE
Sprouts	5–7 days	45–75°F
Microgreens	10–21 days	45–75°F
Stems and leaves	25–60 days	45–75°F
Roots	30–90+ days	45–75°F
Small fruit	75–90 days	65–85°F+
Large fruit	90–120+ days	65–85°F+
Seeds	100+ days	75°F+

Nutrients

You now know plants can feed themselves. But what exactly are these plants eating?

The key nutrients plants need at each stage of growth should ideally be found right where they're planted: in the soil itself. You can ensure your plants get off to a great start by giving them the best, most nutritious soil possible.

For most plants in the garden, I recommend a variation of "sandy loam" (that is, soil made of sand, silt, and clay) that I call *the 103*. (Turn to page 69 for more about this blend.) Throughout this book, you'll learn how to vary the sandy loam blend to incorporate more compost, more sand, or more topsoil, depending on what step you're on in the LRF system.

Once you create the initial soil for your plants to grow in, your job isn't done. Remember the dynamic nature of plants. For every day plants grow a little bigger, the soil grows a little more depleted.

For plants grown on the first two steps, you won't need to worry much about adding nutrients. But the longer and larger your plants grow, the more nutrients they'll need to make it to the finish line.

There are dozens of nutrients plants need to thrive, but we'll focus on the essential soil-derived elements that gardeners refer to as the three primary macronutrients (nitrogen, phosphorus, and potassium), plus a few secondary macronutrients.

Nitrogen for plants is like protein for animals. It's important for good stem and leaf growth. But if a plant has too much nitrogen, it will focus only on growing leaves and neglect forming fruit.

Phosphorus plays a huge role in growing roots and forming flowers and fruit. This nutrient enables a plant to convert sunlight into carbohydrates.

Potassium is key for root and seed production. Potassium helps plants tolerate extreme temperatures. Too much potassium prevents absorption of other minerals like magnesium and calcium.

Beyond these primary three, other important macronutrients include calcium, sulfur, and magnesium. Calcium fortifies plant tissues, helps transport nutrients throughout the plant, and neutralizes acidity both within the plant and in the surrounding soil. Plants need calcium to build strong cell walls and healthy roots. Sulfur and magnesium give flowers and fruit their flavor and leaves their healthy green color.

There's lots more that could be said about plant nutrients, but the good news for gardeners is that 90 percent of the nutrients plants need to stay healthy and productive can be provided by means of organic compost and a little extra dose from one of the nutrients on the chart on page 27.

Water

By now you've selected the most well-lit location, set up the perfect space, timed your planting, and added great soil. Water is the next factor to consider.

Yes, plants can feed themselves, but they can't do so without water. Nutrients like nitrogen, phosphorus, and potassium are absorbed by plants only when dissolved in water. Water and minerals enter a plant through the roots, and water transports nutrients through the plant in a process called transpiration. And much of that water—up to 98 percent in some plants—eventually exits through the leaves by means of transpiration. As water evaporates, it helps a plant maintain its proper temperature. This is why consistent watering is important.

A plant works hard to move water from its roots to its top leaves, branches, and flowers. So the bigger the plant you grow, the more water it'll need.

Not just for food delivery, water also makes plants strong. Without enough water in the cells, the leaves droop. (Tell me I'm not the only one who's seen this

NUTRIENT NEEDS AT EACH STEP

STEPS/STAGE OF GROWTH	IMPORTANT NUTRIENTS	FERTILIZER OPTIONS
1: Sprouts	Nitrogen (though adequate levels of all nutrients are critical at this phase)	Cottonseed meal, alfalfa meal, chicken or rabbit manure, coffee grounds, feather meal
2–5: Leaves, stems, and roots	Root-supporting nutrients like phosphorus and potassium	Kelp meal, greensand, rock dust, coffee grounds, wood ash
6–8: Flowers	Phosphorus, potassium, and calcium	Rock dust, fish bone meal, bone meal, bat guano, chicken and rabbit manure
6–8: Fruit	Phosphorus and potassium	Bone meal, bat guano, fish bone meal, seaweed

happen.) Water gives the plant structure and strength to support its own weight.

As you'll see in the chapters ahead, with each new step in the garden, plants' watering needs increase.

Whether your plants need 1 inch or 4 inches of water per week, consistency in delivering that water is key. Rainwater is best, so track your weekly rainfall, and capture as much rainwater as possible in a rain barrel or large bucket. Each week when there's no rain, it'll be up to you to deliver supplemental water to your plants by watering by hand with a hose or watering can, connecting your garden to a spigot, or installing a formal irrigation system.

Strive to water in the early mornings so that plant foliage has time to dry out throughout the day, and aim the water on the roots, not the leaves. If you use a hose, select the setting on your spray attachment that imitates soft raindrops.

A spigot connection with a drip hose and timer is a great automated setup if you don't have a formal irrigation system. Your plants will get consistent water, and the timer can easily be adjusted as needed. Most hardware stores have drip-irrigation kits available.

Alternatively, a formal irrigation system connects water lines to your home's vacuum breaker and a timer to deliver water at specific times and intervals throughout the week.

Know that your watering system will have to be adjusted as you move through the seasons or if you notice issues, such as the garden surface looking dry or plant leaves that are cracked or wilted. Taking care of the watering is a key way to make sure your plants can take care of themselves.

Care

Now you know: plants know how to grow. They feed themselves, they're tough, they can't walk but still know how to travel, and they can reproduce themselves again and again.

So what could they possibly need from you? Set your plants up for success and they won't need much.

If you follow this book's plan for setting up each plant in the way it grows best, you'll find that tending your plants isn't stressful. In the same way that the needs for space, sunlight, and water increase as you go up each step in the garden, the needs for tending grow as your plants do.

To grow sprouts (Step 1), it's a simple matter of rinsing the seeds a few times a day. But to harvest small fruit (Step 6), plan on pruning, fertilizing, trellising, and fighting off pests. Don't worry: you'll be ready for that responsibility once you get there.

You can expect to spend an hour per week when growing fruiting plants and just a few minutes per week, mostly for harvesting, when simply growing leaves. There's a plant for every schedule—even the really busy ones.

Beyond choosing the best planting setup (which I'll detail in each chapter), care for each plant consists of maintaining the right inputs. This includes ensuring plants' leaves are getting enough sunlight, being certain plants have plenty of space to spread out, taking care that plants never dry out or stay soaked, and, finally, adding extra nourishment to the soil when you know plants need a nutritional boost to make it to the next stage.

Your main job is to be sure each plant has what it needs to do its job. Young plants, old plants, and plants suffering from disease or stress will demand a little more from you, mostly in the way of protection from pests.

"Stay on the offense" is my theory on tending plants. In other words, focus on the positive inputs you bring to the garden rather than dwelling on the negative. The premise is simple: a little positive attention goes a long way.

Here are three key ways to stay on the offense.

Work with nature through an ecosystem. When your garden has a need, before you step in to make a change, first think of a way nature could provide the solution. Does your garden have water runoff problems? Add rain gardens to absorb the excess water. Are your

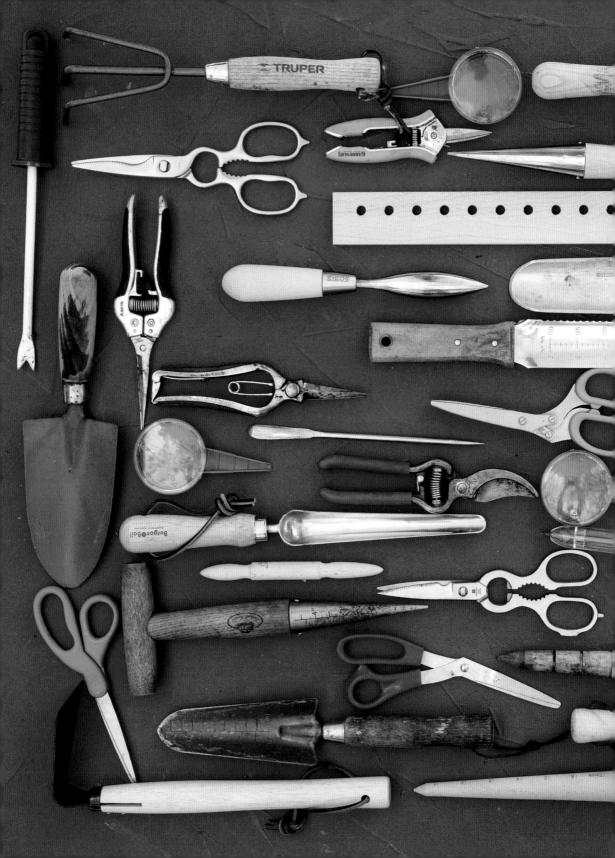

My Favorite Garden Tools

Here are a few of the most-used tools in my gardening bucket.

Hori hori knife. This little gem is three tools in one. Its spike-like tip breaks ground easily. Measurements along one side of the blade indicate how deep you're planting. Its serrated edge can cut a stem or a piece of twine. When you're transplanting seedlings, a hori hori makes it easy to dig small holes in the soil without disturbing neighboring plants.

Dibber. This pointed tool, which is pushed into the soil to produce nice, tidy holes, is my go-to tool for planting seeds. Look for a dibber with inches marked on the side to help measure planting depth.

Needle-nose pruner. This tool's narrow tip lets you get into a plant's interior to cut just where you want and to harvest carefully.

Seed-spacer ruler. The holes on this tool make seed sowing easy. You'll be confident that plants will have the room they need to grow to their fullest potential.

Spray bottle. This is perfect for quickly spraying plants with compost tea or foliar feed for a nutrient boost, or with liquid garlic barrier when leaves are getting munched on by a pest.

Twine and scissors. Use twine to tie up vining plants or lend support to bush varieties without damaging precious stems and leaves. Use the scissors to cut twine or snip some leaves for dinner.

plants frequently damaged by wind? Add trees or shrubs to form a windbreak. Bring in flowers and native plants so there are more beneficial insects and pollinators in the garden. Install a water feature so animals don't come looking for water among your fruit. And when there's a pest issue, consider what prey animal you could attract to control the pest or if you could offer the pest something else found in nature to distract it from your garden. Working with, not against, nature in the garden through an ecosystem is key for garden care.

Check on plants regularly to prune, harvest, or clean. Consistency in tending to your plants is key to less stress. If you schedule a few minutes with your plants each day, you'll notice when one could use a little more water, pruning, or nutrients. You'll be able to tend as needed, right away, before larger problems develop.

Use protective covers. Pests, big and small, have their eyes on your garden. The simplest, most effective way to protect your plants from pests is with protective covers—things like cloches to protect greens from rabbits, hoops and mesh netting to block small insects, hardware cloth cages to protect fruit from squirrels or birds, hardware cloth lining on the bottoms of beds to prevent underground rodents from digging

A System Inside a System: Using Native Plants

Native plants are simply plants that are indigenous to the region, meaning the plants grow naturally and wildly there without the help of people. Adding native plants around your landscape and garden is the perfect way to work with nature. Because natives are accustomed to your climate, they need less water and tending. Most natives are drought tolerant and pest resistant. If these plants can survive the wild, you know they're tough. Native plants also provide habitat for your local animal species, and their shadows are often the only places where these creatures nest and raise their young.

Once you plant natives, you can expect a return of toads, frogs, insects, birds, bees, and butterflies to your space as well. These creatures bring a complete system of prey and predator to your garden that slowly but surely can even out the score on pest pressure you may currently experience in the garden. And bees and butterflies are pollinators, so their increase in the garden means an increase in fruit production too.

So as you add new plants to your garden with each new step in your garden journey, be sure to add some new native plants too.

into the garden, and, when necessary, a tall fence around the garden to protect plants from large pests like deer.

Even when you are on the offense, though, pests and disease may still find a way in. You'll know that pests like caterpillars, borers, beetles, aphids, grasshoppers, flies, mealybugs, slugs, and whiteflies have found the weakest plants in your garden when you spot holes in leaves or fruit. Disease is usually evident from changes in the color or texture of leaves, stems, or fruit.

It's best to act at the first sign of attack. But before reaching for a harsh spray, try a simple tool first: a clean pair of pruners. Prune away damaged and

discolored leaves on the plant. Check the soil area and the undersides of leaves, where pests like to hide. If you spot a pest, toss it into a bowl of soapy water. Once you've cleaned around the plant, add some fresh compost.

Watch the plant that is under attack for a couple of days. If treatment is necessary, the goal is to be as gentle as possible. Spraying with an insecticidal soap will typically take care of most insects. If that doesn't work, you can apply garlic oil spray. For caterpillars, there's Bt spray. For slugs and snails, there's diatomaceous earth. But sprays and solutions are definitely a last resort.

I've found that getting the setup right in my garden space and checking on the plants regularly goes much further than sprays and soaps in keeping pests at bay.

The Steps Ahead

Now that you're all set up and acquainted with the LRF system, it's finally time to start growing leaves, roots, and fruit.

Here's a road map of the journey ahead.

In Steps 1 through 3 of this book, you grow leaves. The first steps focus on plants you'll grow for leafy harvests including sprouts, herbs, and salad greens. Plants grown for their leaves can produce a harvest in as few as 5 to 21 days between 45 and 75°F, with 4 hours of sunlight per day, and in just 1 square foot of space.

Plants featured in Steps 4 through 5 will be grown for their roots. These plants require 35 or more days, at least 6 sunlight hours, and a little more space in the garden.

The fruit appears in Steps 6 through 8 on plants that require at least 75 and as many as 150 or more days of growing time, more than 8 hours of sunlight daily, and 2 or 3 (or more) square feet of space.

Each time you take a new step up in the garden, you'll step up the amount of resources you give the garden too.

You don't have to follow the LRF system exactly. But as soon as you catch on to the connection between what your plant produces and what your plant needs, you'll no longer have to guess at your garden success. All you have to do is grow with your plants.

And even though we start with just one small step, you're still going to need a really big bowl.

part two **leaves**

Unless you live in a desert, you probably walk by billions of the most magical things in the universe every day and don't even realize it.

Leaves.

Even as I write this, I can look out my window and see millions of blades of grass. Thousands of tiny leaves are waving in the wind on just one maple tree. And out in my kitchen garden, there are more leaves than I can count.

Perhaps we take leaves for granted because they're so common. We don't appreciate how magical they are and that they're so good for us, for our gardens, and for the whole planet because everywhere we turn, there they are.

Not to worry. These first few steps will change all that. By the time you finish this section, you will love leaves. You will delight in every leaf you see. You'll appreciate the supernatural event that occurs each time a plant forms this perfect little unit of life. And maybe, just maybe, you'll want to eat more leaves than you ever have before.

Along with roots, leaves are the prerequisite for all other plant growth. Anything we want from a plant, even if it's not the leaves, must come through the leaves to start. So even if you're eventually growing plants for their roots or fruit or seeds, you won't have anything

to eat unless the plants' first leaves thrive. The energy and food that grow all those delicious other plant parts? They come thanks to the leaves.

For many of our veggie plants, every single leaf, including the very first one, is 100 percent A-OK to eat. Leaves from the Brassicaceae (mustard), Amaranthaceae (amaranth), and Asteraceae (aster) plant families are not just edible; they're incredibly nutritious too.

In fact, proponents of sprouts and microgreens argue that the highest level of nutrition is available in the youngest of leaves. You'll never get a more vitamin-packed serving of any edible plant than you will from the first true leaves it grows.

For that reason, we start our gardening journey here, in this place where you've already been but perhaps never noticed before. We begin with the thing that is most available to us, most eager to grow, to spread, and to thrive. We begin with the magic of a green leaf that can harness the rays of the sun, absorb the minerals of the soil and the water in the air, and create its own energy to grow forever and feed us along the way.

STEP 1

Sprouts, Shoots & Microgreens

"I'd love to garden, but I just don't have the space."

I must have said these words a hundred times when I was in my 20s. During those years, I lived in a small apartment in China, a row house in Philadelphia, and a townhome in Virginia. Though my living space increased with every move, I never felt like I had a true "yard" or a spot to put down roots and start growing. I still remember climbing the stairs to my apartment in China and seeing the farmers working the terraced fields behind me. Or driving in from an hour-long commute in Philly and passing my friend as she watered her flowers. For a long time, it felt like gardening was for people with picket fences or a farm. And I wasn't one of those people.

Now, even as I sit here with a larger yard than I've ever had before, it's ironic that I often find as much, if not more, joy in the sprouts I harvest from the kitchen counter and the greens I bring up from the basement as I do in the harvest baskets I fill from my raised beds. If only my current self could've shown my twentysomething self that gardening was less about space and more about perspective. Because I was convinced that I needed a large yard and a dedicated area to truly start gardening, I missed all the opportunities that were right in front of me. Even in my little Chinese apartment, there was room to grow sprouts, microgreens, and a small salad garden. If that space was adequate, then I'm sure you've got enough room right where you are too.

You know the saying "Whether you think you can or you think you can't—you're right"? Well, here's my version: "Whether you think you have enough space to garden or not—you're underestimating."

Perspective matters. If you believe you've got enough space to start growing, then you'll begin where you are and find you have more than you thought. But if you're convinced, as I once was, that what you have isn't enough, then you'll keep finding reasons to wait and miss all the harvest bowls you could already be filling.

So, for a moment, I want you to believe that you already have all you need to become a gardener and grow greens year-round. In this first step, you'll learn what I wish I'd known way back when.

Sprouts and small greens are Step 1 because they introduce you to the basics of plant growth and help you find success almost immediately and in any space. Singing or playing a scale is technically making music (even if it feels basic). Similarly, growing sprouts and greens is truly gardening, even if you only fill one salad bowl with your harvests.

Instead of buying plants, we'll buy seeds. Instead of starting outside, we'll begin inside, on a windowsill or under a simple grow light. And instead of committing to months of waiting for our first harvest, we cut from our garden within days of sowing.

We begin the way our plants begin: with a tiny seed.

Each seed starts a new life cycle when pushed into soil. A sprout is just what it sounds like—the first growth of the plant as the seed pops open, before the true leaves appear. From each seed, growth happens simultaneously, both upward and downward. After the sprout stage, the plant progresses to microgreen status. At this point, the plant has grown beyond its first shoot and root and has started to develop a thicker set of roots, its cotyledon, and then, finally, its first true leaves. A microgreen is harvested before the stem grows very long, and it can be cut either right after the cotyledon or a few days later when the first set of true leaves appears.

Plant Families

You can grow many plants for their sprouts or young greens, but these four plant families comprise the majority of sprouts and microgreens you'll typically want to grow.

Asteraceae. Commonly known as the aster or daisy family, this includes lettuce varieties like buttercrunch, radicchio, endive, romaine, red lettuces—any lettuce that you love can be enjoyed in a much smaller form as a microgreen or sprout. Sunflowers are included in this plant family too.

Amaranthaceae. Plants in the amaranth family—including spinach, Swiss chard, and beets—can all be enjoyed as microgreens or sprouts. If you're looking for sprouts or greens in a rainbow of

colors (especially shades of red, orange, and pink), this family is one to try.

Apiaceae. If you love carrots or parsley or cilantro, growing microgreens from this family is a great way to add those flavors to your dishes without growing large plants in the garden. These sprouts contain all the taste of mature plants but grow in a much smaller and contained space.

Brassicaceae. The brassica, mustard, and leafy green family provides loads of options for sprouts and microgreens: arugula, radish, kale, kohlrabi, turnip greens, mustard greens, mizuna, broccoli, and more. These near-microscopic seeds are fast to sprout and easy to grow as tiny greens any time of year.

Setup

SPACE

Growing plants for sprouts and microgreens harvest is your ticket to the tiniest magic show: a spectacular event that takes place under a big top the size of this book. It's a feat of nature that provides as much nutrition in a few tiny leaves as you could harvest from an entire row of plants—seriously.

All that with just a few minutes of setup or preparation.

Sprouts and microgreens can be grown in a container as small as a dinner plate. For that reason, we'll speak of space needs in terms of how much you can harvest for one serving. These plants are called "micro" for a reason—they really are tiny.

Sprouts do well in a jar or a sprouting tray that has drainage holes or a special serrated top (small enough to keep the seeds in and large enough to let the water out). Alternatively, you can simply use a bowl and a strainer. You'll need a container that allows you to rinse the seeds and then drain them fully again and again during the growing process.

For microgreens, I've found that the ideal container is at least the size of a baking sheet so I have enough for one big salad each time I harvest. The best trays are a couple of inches deep, 12 inches wide, and 18 inches long.

I recommend a container with a minimum volume of ¼ to ½ cubic foot.

To grow sprouts: Begin by soaking a few tablespoons of seeds in water overnight or for up to 12 hours. After soaking, rinse the seeds, strain them, and set them aside on a tray or place them in a jar with a perforated lid, laying the jar on its side so the sprouts can fully drain. Leave the soaked seeds in place (no need to place them under light) and rinse again 6 to 12 hours later. You've now officially set up your sprouts and will only need to continue rinsing and spreading out your seeds until the sprouts are ready. (More on this in the tending section, page 52.)

To grow microgreens: Wet the seed-starting mix well so it is damp to the touch but not dripping when held in your hand. Spread 1 to 2 inches of the damp mix on the tray with drainage holes. Scatter the contents of a seed packet over the tray. You want the seeds to fully cover the soil but not overlap.

Lightly sprinkle ½ inch of the remaining seed-starting mixture over the planted seeds. Set the planting tray on the non-draining tray. Cover the tray with a dome or a tea towel and place it in a cool spot. Check the tray daily to look for signs of growth, noting the soil moisture level and adding water to the nondraining tray if needed. At the first sign of growth, place

the sprouting tray 3 or 4 inches below the grow lights and set the lights to shine on the trays for 12 hours a day.

Voilà! You've officially taken the first step on your garden journey. And you didn't even have to leave the kitchen.

SUNLIGHT

Here's some surprising news: sprouts and microgreens don't need light to begin the growing process. While all plants need sunlight, most seeds germinate in darkness; it's water that wakes them from dormancy.

If you're simply growing sprouts, don't worry about light at all. You can start most seeds in the ambient light—nothing too bright—of your kitchen, and you'll get loads of sprouts 5 to 6 days after soaking.

Microgreens will require light to reach the leafy greens stage rather than stay as sprouted seeds. The initial sprouting can happen in a cool, dark place to imitate a seed germinating underground, but once the first green shoots appear, they grow best with consistent, bright light that's placed 3 to 4 inches above the tray.

You can use a formal grow-lamp setup with lights that can be lowered and raised above the plant trays. This method is more complex to set up but simple to maintain. As the sprouts grow each day, the artificial light is raised so that the bulb never touches the greens but is kept a few inches away.

Microgreens will grow most consistently indoors under a grow light or in a climate-controlled greenhouse outdoors. Microgreens thrive with 12 hours of

The Step-by-Step to Planting Microgreens

1 Gather a seedling tray, a nondraining tray, seed-starting mix, microgreens seeds, and water.

2 Add water to the seed-starting mix until it's moist.

3 Spread the dampened mixture in the seed-starting tray.

4 Scatter seeds evenly on top of the soil mix and lightly cover with compost.

5 Lightly rake the seeds to disperse them evenly.

6 Lightly press the seeds to ensure soil contact.

7 Cover with a dome until the seeds germinate.

8 Place under lights and water the nondraining tray when the soil dries.

artificial light, but if exposed to natural sunlight, they may grow with fewer hours. (I don't recommend growing microgreens on a windowsill as they will produce longer stems and less-robust leaves and will be less productive than those grown under grow lights.)

SEASON

After I gardened in the warm climate of Houston, "shocked" doesn't begin to express my feelings about the winters in Chicago. We landed in the Midwest in the middle of a polar vortex, an experience I'd only recommend for Santa Claus and his reindeer.

Suffice it to say that my first winter in the Midwest was tough. Yes, I was cold, but more than that, I missed gardening year-round and eating the greens that had grown all winter in my southern garden. So after we survived the first winter, I knew I needed a way to find some green through the coldest months.

The following year I gathered my supplies, bought seeds before the holidays, and started planting on January 1. Within weeks, I was cutting microgreens and sprouts nearly every day, even the days when I looked outside and could see nothing but snow.

By February I was eating fresh greens weekly, and the calendar told me the spring solstice wasn't too far away. Winter was still a challenge, but I had found a way to push through the dark and frigid days without hopping on an airplane and flying south.

LIGHT REQUIREMENTS

	SUNLIGHT HOURS	GROW LIGHT HOURS
SPROUTS	0	0
SHOOTS	2–4	6–8
SMALL MICROGREENS	8–10	8–12
LARGE MICROGREENS	8–10	10–12

I'm not saying that growing microgreens is the solution to winter doldrums . . . but I'm not saying it isn't. And speaking of survival, the summers in the Deep South aren't exactly a walk in the park—especially when it comes to keeping plants alive in the garden. Microgreens can be used to stretch the salad garden season during summer as well.

Most microgreens and sprouts grow easily and quickly in typical indoor temperatures between 60 and 70°F. If part of your home runs cooler, they may do even better. For me, a little closet in my basement gives me the most success. In our Houston home, my choice would've been the hall storage closet (without an AC vent) that remained at a constant temperature year-round.

Whether you're surviving a frigid winter or pushing through a scorching summer, mastering Step 1 means you never have to wait for the "right" season to start gardening.

Care

WATER

When you grow sprouts and microgreens, you're cultivating seeds at their earliest stages. As you now know, seeds require water to wake up from dormancy; then they swell and expand rapidly in order to sprout. Once the little plants are growing, water works to distribute their energy and nutrients, so it's critical that the small leaves never lose moisture before you harvest them.

Sprouts should be rinsed with water at least twice a day. To do so, you'll cover all the seeds with water and then let the seeds drain quickly. Each time water washes over a seed, the seed coating dissolves a little more and the seed absorbs more moisture. Within a matter of days, these little bursts of water power the growth of the sprouts.

Shoots and microgreens don't need rinsing. Instead, maintain an even

moisture level throughout the greens tray. These seeds are tiny and just beginning their growth, so it's important not to disturb them in the soil. For this reason, it's best to water from under the plants by setting microgreens on a tray with drainage holes that's placed on top of a tray that doesn't drain.

The need for water for microgreens and sprouts will depend on your setup's temperature and airflow. Don't automate your watering. Instead, touch the soil with your finger daily to check for moisture. If the soil is slightly moist, there's no need to water. If it's dry to the touch, add an inch of water to the bottom tray.

The soil in the top tray will slowly absorb the water throughout the day and release that moisture to the tiny seedlings.

Water is key to the growth of sprouts and greens, but a little goes a long way. Work watering into your daily schedule and you'll never have to worry whether the tiny leaves are drying out.

As long as the light is consistent, successfully growing sprouts and greens depends on your attention to their water needs more than anything else. If the sprouts or microgreens dry out during the growing process, they'll likely wilt or stop growing before you get to eat them. Put simply: drying out equals dying out.

NUTRIENTS

Step 1 is meant to make starting to garden as simple as possible. Speaking of simple, all the nutrition that sprouts and microgreens need to support their growth to this point is already inside the seed itself.

Microgreens benefit from added nutrients only if the growth of the plant seems to slow or if the small leaves change color. If your microgreens show signs of slowing growth, you could sprinkle earthworm castings or a little compost on the soil medium, but be careful not to cover these teeny-tiny plants. I've found that the nutrients within the seeds themselves are more than enough to see the plants all the way through to a healthy harvest, even when I'm growing larger microgreens.

The fact that these small leaves need so little to start growing is good news for your own nutritional needs too. Inside each little sprout are all the nutrients that would eventually be dispersed throughout the mature plant's stems, flowers, and fruit. But because you're just growing a plant to the sprout or micro stage, your body gets to benefit from all those nutrients in just a few bites of greens.

TENDING

If small growing space and easy setup aren't enough to convince you to try these veggies, maybe this fact will: microgreens and sprouts don't need much attention.

Beyond keeping a regular watering schedule, the only other task for tending sprouts is to shift them in their container daily to ensure proper airflow and prevent mold or mildew. I suggest keeping sprouts near your kitchen sink so that tending becomes an easy part of your daily routine. Each time you step up to rinse the dishes, you'll see the sprouts, and you can keep track of their growth, rinse them when needed, and know when they're ready for harvest.

For shoots and microgreens, you're in charge of monitoring the light every day, checking the tray water level, and ensuring that there's equal growth for all the greens. I keep my microgreens in the basement and make it a point to head down there in the mornings and evenings to turn the grow light on and off and to check the water level. If the greens are holding too much water, I turn on a fan. I also run my hands along the greens to help strengthen their roots and shake free any seeds that may be hanging on to the first leaves.

This tending takes 1 or 2 minutes per trip downstairs, so 5 minutes a day at most. Then all that's left is harvesting and starting again.

Small leaves mean small chores. These are tiny tasks you can do in a matter of minutes each day, yet you'll reap platefuls of greens in exchange. Try it and you'll see that a little time can equal loads of high-quality results. Few garden projects will cost you so little in time, space, and money yet give you so much in flavor, nutritional content, and consistent harvests.

Harvest

TIME

Though the tending needs for micro-greens and sprouts aren't much, you may find yourself obsessed with checking in on these tiny plants each day—not because they need your help but because you can't believe how quickly they're changing. These plants double, if not quadruple, in size every day, which means the time when you'll get to eat the fruit—no, the leaves—of your labor is fast approaching. Sprouts can be harvested in 5 to 7 days and microgreens in 10 to 21 days from planting. Harvests come quickly because these leaves are the very start of the plants' lives. If you've been looking for a quick gardening win, this is it.

PRODUCTION

Overheard at the farmers market:

"Twelve ears of corn? That'll be three dollars."

"One watermelon? Four bucks, please."

"A pound of potatoes? That's three-fifty."

"Oh, you'd like to try our micro-greens? That will be a hundred dollars."

I may or may not have exaggerated that last line. But if you've ever shopped for microgreens, I'm sure you'll agree: buying these tiny leaves isn't cheap. In fact, it's likely the highest price you'll pay per pound of produce.

The pricing reflects the logistics required to get these greens to you in a way that you can actually eat and enjoy them. When you purchase microgreens or sprouts, you're not paying so much for the produce but for the growing time, packaging, and transportation. You'll get much more bang for your buck when you skip past the microgreens at the farmers market and grow your own instead.

You can expect one soup-size bowl of sprouts per ½-square-foot tray or one jar filled a fourth of the way with seeds 5 to 7 days after first soaking. And for each square foot of microgreens seeds planted, you can harvest one or two bowls of microgreens within 12 to 24 days.

Those harvests may not seem like much at first, but you'll soon find that in a small space and short time, you're growing sprouts and greens that would otherwise cost $5 to $10 a serving. And you'll enjoy these greens a split second after you cut them, so the taste and nutrition will be exponentially better than what you purchase at the grocery store or farmers market.

This homegrown bounty adds up quickly. You'll soon have your hands and mouth full of so much leafy goodness that you'll feel like a million bucks—or at least a hundred.

Taking This Step

"Will you help me make a video?" I asked my kindergartner in a way that wasn't really a question. I passed her a clear food container, small enough to fit in her little hand. Inside was a jumble of tiny green sprigs.

This container had been sitting on my east-facing kitchen windowsill for the past week, and the microgreens were ready for cutting. I handed my daughter a pair of kindergartner scissors, grabbed my phone, and pressed the camera dot as she carefully held the scissors and slowly cut away at the greens.

As soon as she finished, I posted the video online. The lighting was awful and the videography even more so, but when I checked my phone one last time

The Step-by-Step to Planting Sprouts

1 Gather a draining tray, a nondraining tray, seeds, and water.

2 Place 1 to 2 tablespoons of seeds in the nondraining tray.

3 Soak the seeds for up to 12 hours in water.

4 Place the seeds in a strainer and place in an unlit spot.

5 Carefully spread the seeds evenly on the straining tray.

6 Cover and rinse the seeds twice a day for 5 to 8 days before enjoying.

before bed that night, the response was surprising—*tens of thousands of views*. Although I didn't have a large social media presence at the time, I had been posting hundreds of pictures of the impressive raised-bed kitchen gardens—some more than 250 square feet—I'd worked on for the past couple of years. Yet none of the garden posts had received half the attention of that little harvest of microgreens. As a business owner who knows the importance of marketing and attention, I couldn't help but ask myself why everyone seemed to love *this* video. Was it the tiny hands? The homemade (ahem, terrible) quality of the film?

The answer, I think, was that this video showed there was a lot you could grow (and harvest) in a tiny kitchen container. The kindergartner and shaky videography only confirmed the approachability of this way of gardening. It felt like something everyone watching could do themselves (and everyone was right).

Once you watch a handful of seeds become a jarful of sprouts or toss your first bunch of microgreens into a salad, you might get hooked too. There's something magical about harvesting a homegrown leaf and adding it to your meal, even if you can consume your garden-to-table experience in a single bite.

Sprouts and microgreens are the perfect introduction to gardening. Small leaves are the first step in a plant's growth, so it makes sense to start here.

These leaves aren't needy in terms of space or light; you can grow them nearly anywhere, from basements to sun porches and everything in between, and you'll get your first harvests in a matter of days.

Because you're picking and eating greens at their earliest stages of growth, none of that great nutrition gets lost during transport; these greens go straight from their growing container to your plate.

And because you're gardening inside, you can grow these greens year-round, wherever you live. Whether it's scorching, freezing, or raining cats and dogs outside, you can be in the kitchen with fork in hand, eating yet another round of delicious and nutritious greens every single day of the year.

Growing these tiny leaves has the power to transform you from someone who buys everything you eat into someone who eats something money can't buy. This may be one small step in your garden journey, but it could become one giant leap for you as a gardener.

Now that you've tasted what can happen when you follow the step-by-step system, you will love the flavors you're about to discover in Step 2.

Growing a Daily Supply of Sprouts

SET UP

- Gather the supplies (see page 56).

PLANT

- Soak a few tablespoons of seeds in water for about 12 hours or overnight.

- After soaking, rinse the seeds, drain them, and set them aside on a tray with drainage holes or place them in a jar with a perforated lid, laying the jar on its side to allow extra water to drain off.

- Rinse again 6 to 12 hours later.

TEND

- Continue rinsing and spreading out the seeds every 6 to 12 hours until the sprouts are ready.

- Shift them in their container daily to ensure proper airflow and prevent mold or mildew.

HARVEST

- Give the sprouts a final rinse and shake off any lingering seed coats, then enjoy.

Growing a Daily Supply of Microgreens

SET UP

- Gather the supplies (see page 47).

PLANT

- Wet the seed-starting mix so that it is damp to the touch but not dripping when held in your hand. Spread 1 to 2 inches of the damp mix on a tray with drainage holes.

- Scatter the seeds evenly on the moistened seed-starting mix and cover lightly with ½ inch of the damp mix.

- Cover with a dome or tea towel until the seeds sprout.

- Once the seedlings appear (after 1 to 4 days), uncover the tray and place it under grow lights.

TEND

- Provide 10 to 12 hours of artificial light daily.

- Check the soil moisture daily by touching the soil with your finger. If the soil is slightly moist, there's no need to water. If it's dry to the touch, add more water as needed in the nondraining bottom tray.

HARVEST

- Once the greens have grown their first or second set of leaves, cut the greens just above the soil line.

- Empty the tray and compost the soil.

- Clean and sterilize the tray by soaking it in a mixture of 9 parts water to 1 part vinegar.

- Start again.

Herbs

"I planted some oregano seeds by the front door. Hopefully they'll come up."

Somehow, my mom always knew exactly what I *really* needed any time she came to stay with me.

In this case I'd just had my second baby, and somewhere in the middle of the sleepless nights, diaper changes, and countless loads of laundry, my mom had stepped outside with a packet of seeds and scattered them in my small front garden.

A few weeks later, I sat with my baby boy on the stoop of our townhome, hoping the fresh air would stop the latest crying episode.

And that's when I saw them: sprigs of green peeking out of the soil.

I'm sure that's a weed, I thought to myself. Weeds, after all, were all I'd successfully grown until then. But still, I reached over, gently rubbing the tiny leaves between my index finger and thumb. It was the smell of my mom's kitchen on spaghetti night.

Could this be the oregano she planted? It could be, and it was.

Over the next few weeks, I did nothing to help this oregano plant grow—I gave it no water, apart from what fell from the sky, no protection, no fertilizer. All I offered this plant was the tired but expectant eyes of a new mother. And somehow, that was all it took.

From my stoop, I had a front-row seat to the first plant magic I'd finally sat still enough to observe. One leaf turned into 2, then 10, then 20, then 200, perhaps all the way to 2,000, as the oregano spread and spread in that square-foot spot of my front yard.

Even though I had "no time for a garden," I harvested one handful of oregano after another well into fall that year.

And would you believe it? The following spring, when my son was walking and the piles of snow cleared, those tiny, bright green leaves appeared again, one after the other, popping up as if to say, "Hey there! You loved us so much last year, we thought you'd enjoy an encore."

Each fragrant sprig I cut and tossed onto the spaghetti in my own kitchen offered a subtle hug from my mom any day I needed it. And though I didn't realize it at the time, those tiny cuttings of oregano were my first step to becoming a kitchen gardener.

If you're in a season of life where your hands are too full to add one more thing to your calendar, take a note from my mom and plant some oregano.

That's all you need to do to take the second step in your gardening journey.

Herbs are hardy plants that tolerate minimal maintenance and flourish in small spaces with moderate sunlight. Since most herbs are grown for their leaves, you can harvest from your plants almost as soon as they start growing. Most herbs are cut-and-come-again varieties, meaning the plants can be harvested from dozens of times. Many are perennials, so one plant will last a gardener for years. In fact, many herbs propagate so easily that one plant can turn into dozens of new plants. Did someone say "free plants"? To top it off, herbs are easy to harvest and use fresh, dried, and frozen, meaning gardeners can enjoy fresh harvests in the growing season and preserved harvests in winter. Herbs may be the most generous plants you'll meet: they let you take from them again and again, all while asking for so little in return. In other words: herbs are the perfect plant for a busy gardener.

It's fitting that herbs are Step 2, as we'll focus on two elements for each step in the process:

Two main types of herbs—annuals and perennials, otherwise known as soft and woody herbs (Annuals are planted from seed every year, and perennials either grow year-round in moderate climates or die and grow back from their roots in colder places.)

Two places to grow herbs— indoors and out

Two ways to cultivate herbs—by planting seeds and rooting cuttings

Two ways to use herbs— fresh and dried

Before we dig deeper into all that, let's define "herb."

An herb is any plant with parts (such as leaves, seeds, or flowers) used to flavor food or create medicine.

That chamomile tea you're drinking? It's an herb. That peppermint essential oil? Also an herb. Your sage sticks? Herbs. Bouquet garni? Literally a bunch

of herbs. Pesto? Chimichurri? Tzatziki sauces? All made with herbs.

So why should Step 2 be growing herbs?

Most herbs can grow in a small footprint in your garden, they produce lots of leaves with just 4 hours of sunlight, and many are ready to harvest the minute you purchase or plant them. While sprouts and microgreens are the perfect plants for Step 1 because of their small space needs, herbs are ideal for Step 2 because they almost take care of themselves.

We grow most herbs for their foliage. And since leaves are one of the first things a plant produces, this means you'll be reaping bigger harvests sooner and more often when you grow herbs.

Sounds (and smells) so good, right?

Some herbs are grown specifically for their flowers, such as echinacea, calendula, chamomile, and marigold. We'll touch a bit on flowering herbs in Step 2, but our primary focus is on the leaves because (a) leaves are the simplest thing to grow, and (b) once you've successfully grown an herb's leaves, you're well on your way to getting the flowers too.

Plant Families

Our common household herbs belong to less than ten families in the plant kingdom, but more than 90 percent of these delicious edibles are found in just one plant family.

ROSEMARY

ECHINACEA

CHIVES

TANSY

PURPLE BASIL

DILL

CALENDULA

BAY LAUREL

ITALIAN PARSLEY

SAGE

THYME

MINT

Lamiaceae. This is the biggest family of herbs you'll be growing in your garden. Often called the mint family, it includes common herbs used in everyday cooking—rosemary, lavender, oregano, basil, thyme, sage, winter savory, and, of course, mint.

Most mint-family plants are perennials and classified as woody herbs. They sprout and grow all through the warmest part of the year, produce flowers, slow their growth at the end of the season, and, when frost or snow comes, die back. Once spring arrives and the weather warms, these herbs pop back up from the roots—just like my oregano did that second summer in Virginia.

Basil is an exception. It's an annual. Unlike its perennial cousins, basil grows and produces flowers in one growing season. Inside these blossoms are hundreds of seeds. If you let the herb flower and drop seeds, new basil plants will sprout the following year.

Within this family, thyme and oregano are often the easiest to grow and cultivate through the year, whereas sage and rosemary can be more temperamental. Basil is the easiest to start from seed.

Plants in the Lamiaceae family are remarkable in many ways. For one, you can cut from these plants again and again, and this continuous harvest only spurs the plants to grow more. If you grow nothing else in your garden but these herbs, you'll still have so much to pick and enjoy.

Asteraceae. Another great plant family to grow is the aster—one of the largest plant families on the planet. Asters are also known as the daisy or lettuce family (you'll see this family again in Step 3). Herbs in this family are grown mostly for their flowers. What sets the aster family apart is their formation of beautiful clusters of little flowers at the end of their plant life.

The first herb you might grow from this family is stevia, a natural sweetener for use in tea or lemonade. Chamomile and echinacea are familiar Asteraceae herbs that are great for making fresh or dried teas. Calendula can also be grown to produce teas, tinctures, and infused oils. If you're more of a coffee drinker, the ground, roasted roots of chicory can serve as a coffee substitute, while its leaves can be added to salads.

Yarrow produces gorgeous flowers ideal for making dried wreaths and bouquets. Marigold flowers are both edible and often used for medicinal purposes. Feverfew, marigold's cousin, was traditionally used to treat headaches and fevers (the name fits!). Dandelions are found in this plant family too, and its leaves are known to aid with digestion.

The aster family, with its gorgeous flowers, makes a fantastic addition to your garden, and the herbs are useful in so many ways in the kitchen. While you can use many of the flowers from these plants, the leaves are often edible and full of flavor as well.

Apiaceae. Also known as the carrot or parsley family, this group is best known for its namesake, the carrot. The Apiaceae family includes common kitchen herbs like cilantro, dill, and parsley, along with fennel and cumin.

If you think of this group as the carrot family, you're halfway to understanding the growth habits of these herbs, including their weather, temperature, and soil preferences. Picture a carrot's root system. Most Apiaceae herbs have a similar taproot of some size. The longer these herbs remain in the garden, the bigger their taproots can grow. I've harvested parsley that had been in the garden for a year and a half, and the root structure was nearly 12 inches long.

Herbs in this family are primarily the annual type—growing from seed to seed in one season. The one exception is parsley, which is a biennial and will, with

optimal weather conditions, remain in the garden for two years before producing seeds.

Lauraceae. The laurel family includes bay laurel as well as avocado and cinnamon plants.

Bay laurel provides a deep, savory flavor to culinary dishes that can't be found in other herbs. Laurel is a perennial

HERB FAMILIES AT A GLANCE

FAMILY	COMMON PLANTS
Amaryllidaceae	Onion chives, garlic chives
Apiaceae	Cilantro, dill, fennel, parsley
Asteraceae	Chamomile, calendula, echinacea, marigold
Lamiaceae	Basil, marjoram, mint, oregano, rosemary, sage, thyme
Lauraceae	Bay laurel

that grows much like a bush or tree. Depending on where you live, you might be able to enjoy this as an ornamental bush in your landscape.

Amaryllidaceae. Called the amaryllis or allium family for short, this group covers all things onion: onion sets grown just for the greens, plus shallots, leeks, and chives. You know—those potent flavors, usually grown as bulbs underground, that are the essential start to so many culinary dishes.

I'm not sure everyone considers chives an herb, but when I think about the foods that maximize flavor in the kitchen, chives and green onions are high on my list. That's enough for me to include them in Step 2. You'll learn how to grow onions and garlic in Step 5 when we explore bulbs.

Setup

Oftentimes new gardeners plant an herb directly in the ground in their landscape and start watering every day, envisioning fields of lavender just outside their back door. When the plant turns brown or doesn't seem to grow at all, they're suddenly convinced they'll never have a green thumb. But there's actually nothing wrong with their thumb (or yours).

It's the setup that's the problem. So before you dig in and plant your first herb, consider where these plants initially grew.

Herbs in the mint family, plus bay laurel, originated in the Mediterranean region. The aster family originated in South America, and the Apiaceae family began growing in tropical regions of Southeast Asia and North and South America.

Take a moment to think about the climates in Greece or Chile or the Caribbean. What thoughts pop into your head? Sand? Sun? A little bit of water? Lying on the beach sipping drinks with cute little umbrellas? (Maybe that last one's just me.) Unless your climate and

your native soil are similar to that of these plants' origins, you will have to adapt your garden setup to more closely match that of these herbs' hometowns.

So before we plant herbs, we need the right soil blend. You want well-draining soil so plants don't become waterlogged. I highly recommend making your own blend as opposed to buying a mix from the store. My go-to blend is my version of a sandy loam soil mix. It's basically ⅓ topsoil, ⅓ compost, and ⅓ torpedo or construction sand—plus a few extra magic ingredients. Together they form the perfect organic mix for growing herbs. (See below, Meet Your Ideal Garden Soil: The 103, for more details.)

One of my first efforts at kitchen gardening was a pot of garlic chives on our front porch when the kids were preschoolers and toddlers. During that season, I couldn't keep one room in my house clean for more than five minutes, but I could step outside and harvest chives for a Saturday omelet and feel like Martha Stewart. It whetted my appetite for growing my own fresh food in a simple way, and it only took one terra-cotta pot.

When you're ready to start Step 2, don't forget what's possible with just a few containers. Though herbs need more growing space than sprouts, the amount these plants can produce from just one

Meet Your Ideal Garden Soil: The 103

If you haven't read my first book, *Kitchen Garden Revival*, I'd like to introduce you to the 103, my perfect soil blend. The 103 is a rich soil consisting of 33 percent locally sourced topsoil, 33 percent coarse sand (also called "torpedo" or "construction" sand), and 33 percent finished compost.

The topsoil is a great base that keeps the soil mix fluffy and light, provides structure for your herb garden, and maintains its consistency over a long period of time. Sand helps with drainage. And compost is an excellent addition because it slowly releases lots of nutrients over the plants' season of growth and is rich with organic matter and all kinds of helpful microbes.

This nearly perfect trio brings us to 99 percent of my completed soil blend, but there's just a little something missing to make this soil "103." The bonus 4 percent comes from adding worm castings, chicken manure, or rabbit poop—basically, a substance that's gone through an animal's body and come out the other way. It's this bit of extra over 100 percent that will make your garden more lush and productive.

pot will surprise you. Herbs will grow in a small, confined space, or they'll stretch and take over a larger one, especially if they're perennials. In temperate climates, perennial herbs can keep growing until they become bushes or even small trees. These same herbs planted in climates that experience frost and snow grow about ½ or 1 square foot in size before the growing season ends and they go dormant.

Despite herbs' flexibility, there are ideal spacing recommendations based on plant family.

Plant perennial herbs from the Lamiaceae family no more than 2 per

HERB PLANT NEEDS

FAMILY	SUN	SOIL	WATER	SPACE	TEMPERATURE	DURATION
Carrot (Apiaceae)	4+ hours	Loose sandy loam	Consistent	6–9 per square foot	45–75°F	3–6 months
Daisy (Asteraceae)	4+ hours	Sandy loam with extra nitrogen	Consistent	4–6 per square foot	45–75°F+	3–6 months (echinacea/ rudbeckia is perennial)
Laurel (Lauraceae)	6+ hours	Amended native	Low	1 per 10 square feet	70°F	Perennial
Mint (Lamiaceae)	6+ hours	Sandy loam	Low	1 per square foot	75°F+	Perennial (basil is annual)
Onion (Amaryl-lidaceae)	4+ hours	Loose sandy loam	Low	4–9 per square foot	45–90°F	6–12 months (chives are perennial)

square foot in a container at least 1 foot deep and 1 to 2 feet wide.

Annual herbs in the Apiaceae family, such as parsley and cilantro, will grow taller than wide and can be planted 4 to 6 per square foot. When you're selecting a place to plant these herbs, be aware that they can develop a large taproot. Ideally, you'll need a container or raised bed that's at least 1 foot deep.

Asteraceae plant roots are shallow, and the plants don't take up as much space in the garden as Lamiaceae herbs. A container 6 to 12 inches deep works great for Asteraceae perennials when planted 1 to 2 per square foot.

For the most part, herb plants will grow to the space provided, so it's usually safe to pack plants together. But be ready with your garden scissors if you choose to plant intensively. Be sure you harvest often, at least once a month during the growing season, so one plant doesn't overtake the others.

There are two main ways to create new herb plants: by seed and by cutting. The best method for planting one type of herb isn't necessarily the best way to grow another, and particular plant families generally have a method that works better.

By seed. The best herbs to grow via direct seeding (planting seeds into the garden bed) are typically annuals—those that complete their entire life cycle in a three-month period. Herbs in the Apiaceae family, such as dill, cilantro, and parsley, are perfect for direct seeding.

Their seeds are easy to handle and quick to germinate. And Apiaceae herbs grown from seed usually outperform those brought in as plants from a nursery, because when you plant from seed you don't disturb the plants' taproots during the transplanting process.

Flowering herbs in the Asteraceae family—marigolds, calendula, chamomile, and yarrow—can be started from seed but do best as transplants, meaning you start the seeds indoors and transplant the seedlings into your garden when conditions are optimal. If you started these seeds outdoors, your growing season might not be *quite* long enough for the plants to flower as much as you'd like. By starting seeds indoors, you begin the leafing process earlier and see flowers weeks, if not months, sooner than you would have otherwise.

The seeds of flowering herbs are a little larger and easier to manage than seeds in the mint family, and I've found that most of them are quick to germinate. Plan to start most of these seeds as early as 45 days before you want to set the transplants outdoors.

By cutting. Some herbs are grown through propagation, meaning you cut a piece from a mature plant and encourage that cutting to develop roots and become a mature plant. African blue basil is one such herb. Perennial plants in the Lamiaceae family (such as rosemary, oregano, sage, thyme, and mint) produce roots quickly when cuttings from tender green stems are placed in water or damp coarse sand.

Propagating plants is one of the most magical things you can do in the garden and also one of the best ways to turn one plant you love into a hundred more. But sometimes it's more efficient to head to the nursery and purchase a propagated plant from your best local grower. Buying plants is the more expensive way to start an herb garden, but you save

The Step-by-Step to Potting Up Basil

1 Gather basil, a larger pot, compost, weed barrier cloth, and a nondraining tray.

2 Place the weed barrier cloth at the bottom of the pot.

3 Fill halfway with a compost/sand soil blend.

4 Quickly remove the basil from its original container.

5 Gently divide the basil stems, being careful not to tear the roots.

6 Lay out the basil plants in the larger pot.

7 Use a dibber or trowel to dig holes wide enough to not disturb the roots.

8 Carefully place each basil plant inside each hole.

9 Place the pot on a patio with 4 to 6 hours of sunlight and water regularly.

time and will be on your way to your first harvests in a matter of days.

THE STEP-BY-STEP TO
Propagating Herbs

1   Use clean pruners to cut in a diagonal direction just above a leaf node (where new leaves grow) on a stem that is flexible and not yet woody (these are called soft cuttings).

2   Strip the bottom leaves from the stem, leaving five or six sets of leaves on the upper stem.

3   Dip the stem in cinnamon and/or rooting hormone and place it in a container of organic potting soil or coarse sand.

4   Keep the cutting well watered but not soaking wet.

5   When you see new growth on the tip of the cutting, gently remove the plant from the container and transfer it to a larger pot.

6   Move the plant in and out of the sun for 1 to 2 weeks to help the plant adjust to being outdoors (this is called hardening off) before transplanting it to a raised bed or large container.

7   Water the transplant well and tend it carefully for the first 2 weeks of outdoor growth.

SUNLIGHT

Herbs will take as much sunlight as you can give them. They'll produce more leaves when they receive 4 to 8 hours of sun per day, although most will grow in light on the lower end of that spectrum.

Of all the herbs, rosemary, oregano, and basil need the most direct light. Grow these in a spot that receives sun nearly all day long. Sage, thyme, and mint will manage with semi-shade or part sun.

Asters and alliums are more flexible and forgiving with their light requirements. They thrive with lots of sun but also grow well in part shade. Similarly, Apiaceae herbs perform with just 4 or so hours of sunlight; they are perfect for lower-light areas of your landscape.

SEASON

Herbs are motivated to grow not just by sunlight but by temperature and length of day. Lamiaceae herbs, for instance, tend to love long and warm days (75°F and above), while Apiaceae herbs thrive in cooler temperatures (45 to 75°F).

Basil can take the heat—the warmer, the better—but will die at the first sign of frost. Most of its Lamiaceae cousins, especially plants like winter savory, can withstand temperatures below freezing for a bit. These plants may still look green but will halt their growth and die back during the coldest part of the winter season. Then, as temperatures warm in spring, these perennials send up new stems and leaves from the roots and start flourishing again.

Herbs in the aster family savor the cool season; in fact, they do better when started in cooler weather. These herbs tolerate colder temps in early spring, and many flowering asters produce through the summer, but they won't survive a hard frost.

Plants in the Apiaceae family germinate best when started in cooler weather and perform best in typical spring and fall conditions, when temperatures stay under 75°F. You can sow these seeds in spring as soon as the soil can be worked, even if there's still a slight chance of frost. Toward the end of their life cycle or when the weather warms too quickly, Apiaceae plants will "bolt," producing a thick center stem and a set of flowers in a formation that closely resembles that of an umbrella. The flowers will eventually dry and become seed for next year's plants. Once the herb bolts, you can still eat every part of it, but the flavor changes considerably.

Parsley is an exception here. Technically a biennial plant, meaning it leafs out in the first year and flowers the second, parsley can last in the garden for several years if weather permits. (I've had the same parsley plants in my kitchen garden for nearly three years.) For this reason, don't remove parsley at the end of the season unless it clearly has dried up or gone to seed.

Apiaceae and Asteraceae plants finish in the hottest part of the growing season, but most can be resown for a second round of growth in the cooler weather toward the autumn equinox. In fact, in mild climates you can plant another

round of annual herbs almost as soon as the previous season's plants die off.

In cooler zones with a period of frost or snow, many Lamiaceae herbs can be potted up and moved indoors before the cold air settles in. The herbs won't necessarily produce lots of new leaves indoors, but many plants will continue moderate growth if you keep the soil moist and place them in the sunniest spot you have in your home. I've found the most success with bringing sage, rosemary, thyme, and lavender inside. When the ground thaws in spring, I move these plants back outdoors where they pick up speed and start growing quickly again.

Bay laurel, in the Lauraceae family, is a tropical plant that's happiest in warm weather. It, too, can be potted and brought indoors in cold climates. In mild climates where there's little to no threat of frost, bay laurel can grow as trees or bushes in the permanent landscape. I planted three or four bushes in my Houston yard that grew at least a foot taller each year. Not only are the leaves edible, but the plant is a beautiful evergreen year-round. (Your friends and neighbors will have no idea you're growing food in the front yard!)

Care

WATER

With most culinary herbs, the danger lies not in watering too little but in watering too much. In Step 1, you might have been watering sprouts daily, but you shouldn't give the same amount of H_2O to your herbs. Otherwise, you might love your plants to death.

For the most part, herbs prefer sandy, well-draining soil and consistent but not too much water. Before you water plants in the mint family, double-check the soil 1 inch below the surface; if there's *any* moisture in the soil, don't water yet.

Herbs in the Apiaceae family (parsley, dill, and cilantro) and aster-family flowers can accept water more often. Use the 1-inch-per-week rule for these herbs. Asters don't like their roots sitting in water for too long, so even though you can water more often, make sure you have good drainage first.

Use these watering needs to guide you when setting up an herb container or a raised bed. Plant Lamiaceae herbs on

Work with Nature

Herbs grow well with minimal watering, so they're perfect for growing in areas that lack regular rainfall or experience some periods of drought. Most herbs don't have significant pest issues as long as you keep them pruned and healthy. If you do find caterpillars on your parsley, dill, or cilantro, don't disturb them. These are most likely swallowtail or monarch caterpillars that will soon turn into butterflies.

Group your herb plants together and let their natural scents and growth habits benefit one another. Use chives and scallions as natural pest deterrents for the rest of your herb plants. Allow creeping herbs to grow as ground cover below your larger bushy herbs, and let flowering herbs like echinacea and anise hyssop welcome pollinators and beneficial insects to the garden too.

the outside edges, where the soil dries out first, and place other plant families in the interior, where the soil stays moist longer.

NUTRIENTS

Plants grown for leafy harvests need nitrogen in their diet. So the goal with feeding herbs is to look for bright green leaves. When the color changes to yellow or becomes dull or discolored, that's often a sign that nitrogen is lacking. Add some nitrogen to the soil by mixing a little liquid organic fertilizer into the watering can or spritzing the leaves with a diluted liquid organic fertilizer on a regular basis.

Flowering herbs may benefit from an organic phosphorus-rich fertilizer when they are starting to flower. Again, this can be applied to the soil or spritzed on the leaves of the plant just as the stems are beginning to form the small flower buds.

I rarely amend my soil or add new nutrients to my herb gardens. Apart from a quarterly installment of fresh finished compost or a little addition of earthworm castings, I find that my herbs grow well when set up correctly from the beginning with a rich soil that's full of nutrients.

TENDING

It seems too good to be true, but the main tending task for Step 2 is the most rewarding one: harvesting. Picking leaves for dinner actually deters disease and pests and encourages more leaf production.

Let's say that again for the busy people in the back: your main gardening task for Step 2 is to cut your herb plants and use them. And the more you cut, the more you'll get to use.

As you climb the gardening stairs step-by-step, you'll find that those plants on the bottom stairs respond to some

1 HERB WINDOW BOX

2 TOBACCO BASKET
FOR DRYING HERBS

3 PROPAGATION VASE

4 SMALL WATERING CAN

5 GARDEN BROOM

6 WEED BARRIER CLOTH

7 NEEDLE-NOSE PRUNERS

8 HERB DEHYDRATOR

9 HERB HARVEST
SCISSORS

10 HERB PRUNERS

11 HERB GARDEN
SCISSORS

12 OLLA FOR WATERING

TLC, but they're also perfectly happy to keep growing when left alone.

That being said, if you do have the time, your herb plants will respond favorably to a bit of attention. First, keep the soil around them clear of dead leaves and other debris, where pests love to hide. Although herbs are rarely affected by pests, tidying and cleanup make it even less likely.

Second, prune regularly by pinching soft stems with your fingers or cutting thicker stems with a clean pair of snips.

Pruning, when it comes to herbs, is basically the same thing as harvesting. Cut first from the outermost branches and work your way in. Regular harvesting allows air to flow around plants, preventing mildew and keeping them healthy.

If you're growing an herb for its leaves and it starts to flower, prune the flowers before they bloom. This directs the plant's energy to leaf production instead of flower formation. At the end of my annual herbs' growing season, however, I love to let a few plants bolt

Herb Focus: Mint

Mint is one of the easiest herbs to grow. In fact, it's so easy to grow that I recommend growing it away from other plants (meaning not in your raised beds) because it doesn't always play nicely with others.

You can buy a mint plant or start your own from a rooted cutting. Propagating this herb is possibly the easiest magic trick you'll ever learn. If you take cuttings of mint, you'll notice how quickly its roots, called runners, spread out. Mint likes to take up a lot of space, and its roots will elbow their way past whatever other plants are in their way.

Plant your mint plant in its own container in a spot that isn't too sunny—4 to 6 hours of sun is plenty—and give it about 1 inch of water per week. If the leaves turn brown, the herb either needs more shade or more water. If the leaves turn yellow, you're overwatering.

To ensure bushy plants and plentiful harvests, prune the stems just above a leaf node every few weeks.

and go to seed as a gift to the garden's pollinator insects and birds. And if I get new herbs sprouting from seed next year, that's a bonus.

Harvest

TIME

When will an herb be ready for harvest? That depends on how and when it was planted.

Perennial herbs purchased from a local garden center—like mint, rosemary, oregano, and thyme—can be harvested the very day you bring them home. When I walk new gardeners through a freshly installed kitchen garden, we usually bring along a pair of scissors to cut the very first sprigs of herbs right then and there.

If you propagate herbs from cuttings, allow 4 to 6 weeks for enough roots to form to be ready to plant. Then factor in another 4 to 6 weeks before the rooted plant has grown enough to harvest from.

Annual herbs like parsley, cilantro, and dill seeded directly in the garden take 45 to 60 days. Their soft leaves and stems need time to grow strong before they're worth harvesting. In total, these herbs last 90 to 120 days in the garden. They are sensitive to temperature and day length and will bolt when conditions are no longer optimal for their growth. For that reason, it's critical with annual herbs to take clippings often and to continually plant new seeds during the growing season to ensure you have a harvest for as much of the year as possible.

Bay laurel is slow growing and will need not only plenty of space to grow but also plenty of time. You can still harvest from the plant regularly, even as you give it many seasons to grow tall and add more leaves.

PRODUCTION

A year-round supply of herbs is what you can expect from your Step 2 garden. Once you start growing your own herbs, you'll see why.

If you're in a temperate climate, you can enjoy freshly cut herbs every month of the year; if you're in a cold climate, you can have fresh herbs for half the year (while they grow outside), a few more harvests from indoor-grown plants, and dried or preserved herbs (see page 82) for any months your plants aren't actively growing.

Once an herb plant has produced 5 to 10 main stems, you can expect to harvest from each plant weekly (and you should). The more you cut from the herbs, the more they'll produce.

From one basil plant, I cut at least one or two stems a week. From perennial herbs, I cut three stems per week, and from soft herbs like cilantro and dill, I can cut one to three stems each week during their optimal growing time.

When you're harvesting herbs, cut from the outermost branches and work your way in.

To dry perennial herbs, pick a day or time when the plants' leaves are dry. Cut the stems at the base or just above a leaf node if there's time for the plant to keep growing in the current season. Strip the stem of the bottom few leaves, then tie a cluster of stems together, and hang the bunch upside down for 2 to 3 weeks in a cool, dry, and somewhat dark place (bright sunlight can bleach the greens and remove some of the vibrant herb flavor you're hoping to keep). Once dried, strip the leaves from their stems and store in an airtight jar until you're ready to use.

To preserve annual herbs—most of which don't dry well—chop the leaves, mix with olive oil, and freeze in small units (an ice cube tray works great). Alternatively, just chop and freeze dry in an airtight freezer bag.

As you move through the seasons each year, there's an herb to harvest from the beginning of the growing season to the very end and beyond. Here's what a year-round supply of herbs looks like:

As soon as the weather begins to warm and spring approaches, you cut your first sprigs of perennial herbs like chives, oregano, and thyme that have come back from last year. You continue to harvest these as you see growth from perennial herbs in the aster family like echinacea and as you plant out annual seeds for parsley, dill, cilantro, chamomile, and calendula (you'll begin harvesting these within a few months).

With a young bay laurel, harvest just a leaf or two at a time to avoid overwhelming the plant. Eventually your plant will grow large enough to handle a lot more harvesting. In warm climates, you'll be able to cut off several large branches at a time and then hang them to dry.

Enjoying herbs fresh is a culinary treat, but drying and storing them doubles the amount of time you get to enjoy homegrown tastes. The culinary pros say that, per serving, dried herbs have a stronger flavor than fresh. You'll find this to be true when you dry your own, as the leaves and stems shrink quite a bit. Perhaps it's not that the flavor is stronger; it's just that the plant is more condensed. (Food for thought!)

In the height of the growing season, you harvest mint-family herbs almost daily, from both the perennial plants and the basil you planted by seed. Soon seeds of early-spring annuals like dill and cilantro can be replanted for a fall harvest.

Just before frost and cold weather return, you gather all the herbs you can, enjoy many of those fresh, freeze some, and hang the rest to dry. You transfer some plants to pots to bring inside. During the coldest part of the year, you enjoy the dried and frozen herbs and keep picking from those plants you repotted and brought indoors.

Before you know it, the weather is warming again, and the chives and oregano are just poking their first greens out of the dark, cool soil. The whole process begins again. Suddenly, year-round homegrown herbs aren't just an idea: they are sitting on your plate, topping your favorite dishes, and brewing in your cup of tea every day, 365 days a year.

No More Grocery Herbs:
Take the Gardenary Challenge

One part of Gardenary's mission is to have no more trucked herbs, meaning every single family will be growing and sharing their own herbs within their communities so grocery store herbs (both fresh and dried) are no longer necessary.

Grocery store herbs often travel more than 1,500 miles before reaching our plates, they're covered in single-use packaging, and they lose most of their nutritional value and great flavor in the transportation and packaging process. Because most herbs are leaves, they have a short shelf life. This means most herbs are processed, trucked, packaged, and sold, only to be tossed in the trash because they spoil before we can use them.

By planting your own herbs, harvesting often, and sharing the harvests, you can change the world for the better and make your food more delicious in the process.

Will you join us? You can sign up for the No More Grocery Herbs Challenge at https://gardenary.com/herbgarden. Or you can simply follow the No More Grocery Herbs planting plan:

Grow 1 perennial Lamiaceae plant per person (rosemary, thyme, oregano, sage, mint).

Grow 5 annual Apiaceae plants per person, and keep planting throughout the season (cilantro, dill, parsley).

Grow 2 chives and scallion plants per person.

Grow 1 Asteraceae perennial plant per household (chamomile, echinacea, calendula).

Harvest from the plants weekly during their optimal growing season. Use half the harvest fresh. Dry or freeze the rest of the harvest to use during the off-season.

Taking This Step

Beyond ease of growth, a huge reason to plant more herbs is because of their ROI. You knew your garden was an investment, right?

Mel Bartholomew, an engineer who brought his methodical prowess to the hobby gardener, followed up his book *Square Foot Gardening* (perhaps the best-selling gardening book of all time) with *Square Foot Gardening High-Value Veggies*. In a follow-up book, he uses a simple calculation to determine the ROI on planting particular vegetables and plants per square foot given their predicted amount of harvests.

To most readers' surprise, including mine, the 14 (*14!*) most valuable vegetables to grow in the kitchen garden aren't vegetables at all.

They're herbs.

Though I'm not one to promote gardening as a way to save money, I am *all* about the bragging rights that come from getting a good bargain. And the numbers are clear—the best way to do that in your garden is by growing as many herbs as you possibly can.

Since the grandfather of hobby gardening did the math for us, we should take a minute and be sure our garden harvest adds up too. If you want to grow something that's worth your while and every square inch it takes up in the garden, you'll grow herbs—and a lot of them!

You may only be on the second step of your garden journey, but growing a year-round supply of organic, delicious herbs is no small matter. Even if you stop at this step and remain an herb gardener for life, you'll still accomplish the "garden-to-table" experience, have something you can add to dishes nearly every day of the year, and find yourself with handfuls of happiness you can keep to yourself in the midst of a busy season or share with others to help them through theirs. Herbs are the kitchen gardener's most generous gift that never stops giving.

Growing Herbs

SET UP

- Create a sandy loam soil blend (see page 69).

- Prepare a raised bed; a container with drainage holes; or mounded, amended soil (if planting in the ground).

- Select a spot with 4 to 8 hours of sunlight.

PLANT

- Direct seed annual herbs at 1 to 4 seeds per square foot.

- Plant 1 or 2 perennial plants per square foot.

TEND

- Add an organic source of nitrogen when needed to boost leaf growth (compost is easiest).

- Water consistently, but let the plants dry out between watering.

- Prune the outer and lower leaves often.

HARVEST

- Cut from the outermost branches and work your way in.

- Harvest frequently to encourage more leaf production.

- Use the harvests fresh, or dry or freeze for future use.

STEP 3

Salad Greens

When I first started Gardenary, I was far from being a "gardening pro." I didn't have a degree in horticulture. I hadn't even won Yard of the Month in my neighborhood. I declared myself a "garden consultant" even when I was a long way from knowing how to grow everything in the garden. (Just between us, I still don't know everything!)

But before you call the garden police on me, let me explain. When I met with my first clients, I never promised I could teach them *everything* about gardening.

I didn't have to. I filled our hour together by talking about the thing I *did* know how to do, my favorite aspect of gardening—setting up an organic salad garden.

As a self-taught gardener, I knew that learning everything at once wasn't possible or even enjoyable. Instead, the key to continuing to pick up the trowel season after season is gradually mastering one plant type at a time and incorporating it into your everyday routine.

I knew that if I could help someone quickly grow and harvest delicious salads every week for dinner for half of the year, they'd be on their way to becoming garden pros themselves. Spoiler alert: my plan worked!

This promise of six months of salad greens is no small thing. Picture that plastic box of spring mix you pay $6 for after it's been shipped across the country. Now compare that to a garden bed of sweet, crunchy, and fresh lettuce greens you can harvest right outside your back door.

When you weigh the costs of store-bought greens (like fuel usage, single-use plastics, waste, and the history of widespread E. coli and salmonella outbreaks)

against the benefits of homegrown (vibrant flavor, nutritional content, and access to tasty varieties not commercially available), the garden beats the grocery store in every way (though the grocery variety does have more frequent flyer miles).

"You've spoiled me," my client Reed said. "I can't buy lettuce from the store anymore—it's either from my garden or I can't bring myself to eat it."

I had to confess: "That's exactly what I was hoping would happen." Getting hooked on something so good for you, so good for the planet, and so easy to grow is the best insurance that you'll never stop growing.

If you're still not sure this gardening thing is for you, let me introduce you to salad gardening. Let's pretend it's you and me during one of my first garden consults; I'll tell you how excited I am about my own lettuce garden and see if I can't convince you to start growing your own greens too.

Just don't be mad if you can't bring yourself to buy lettuce from the store anymore either.

Plant Families

Pop quiz time. You've got 10 seconds to name as many salad plants as you can.

Iceberg, one. Romaine, two. Spinach, three. Cabbage, four. Did you think of any others?

If variety is the spice of life, it's clear why some people are not that excited about salads. The truth is there are dozens, if not hundreds, of different plants that produce leaves perfect for tossing into bowls of fresh greens. It's not the

SALAD GREENS FAMILIES AT A GLANCE

FAMILY	COMMON PLANTS
Aizoaceae	New Zealand spinach
Amaranthaceae	Spinach, Swiss chard, beet greens
Asteraceae	Romaine, iceberg, spring mix, radicchio, butterhead, buttercrunch, endive
Basellaceae	Malabar spinach
Brassicaceae	Arugula, kale, radish greens, mustards, cabbage, bok choy, collards, mizuna
Polygonaceae	Sorrel
Tropaeolaceae	Nasturtiums

'BLUE CURLED SCOTCH' KALE

BUTTERCRUNCH LETTUCE

MALABAR SPINACH

'BRIGHT LIGHTS' SWISS CHARD

'BLOOMSDALE' SPINACH

'TOSCANO' KALE

plants' fault that our salad needs so much dressing to add a little flavor; it's our food system.

There are so many more greens worth eating than are stocked at the grocery store. You rarely see these other cultivars on the shelves because they don't ship well or hold up in storage.

So before you dig in and grow your own salad greens, let's meet up with the varieties possible. Three key salad green plant families are the most important to understand.

Asteraceae. First up is the aster family that you met in Steps 1 and 2, which includes the sunflowers, zinnia, marigold, and, of course, aster. But the asters we welcome now are the ones that become delicious salad greens: romaine, iceberg, spring mix, radicchio, butterhead, and buttercrunch. These greens generally prefer the cool season, when temps range from just above freezing to 65 or 75°F.

Brassicaceae. The next plant family is the "dark greens" or mustard family. These salad greens are darker in color than the asters, and they vary in size from small arugula leaves to kale that can grow more than 5 feet in height. The key brassicas in the salad garden include arugula, radishes (grown for their greens), kale, collards, mustards, and cabbage.

These greens prefer the cool season. Brassica plants are frost tolerant if not frost resistant, meaning they can be planted as soon as the soil can be worked in spring and will even grow under frost cloth or a cold frame deep into winter. Some brassicas (namely arugula and kale) can continue growing in warmer weather that exceeds 75°F. Kale and collards are biennial plants, so they can actually make it through two years in the garden if conditions are optimal.

Amaranthaceae. You met the amaranth family in Step 1, but now we grow these family members to their full size. Amaranth favorites for the salad bowl include spinach, Swiss chard, and beets (grown for the leaves). These greens are packed with antioxidants and vitamins, and they also love the cool season. Swiss chard is also a biennial and can last for years in the kitchen garden.

If you were to grow only these three plant families in your kitchen garden, you'd still have way more variety in your salad bowl than you thought possible. Asters, brassicas, and amaranths together produce the majority of the green leaves you can harvest for just-picked salads from the garden for much of the year, if not year-round, since each family includes plants that can withstand frost and some that can survive summer's hottest temperatures.

After you master plants in these three families, you can expand to less-well-known plant families, especially when you're ready to grow into the heat of the summer. For warmer times of year, the Tropaeolaceae family includes nasturtium, a peppery green that produces beautiful edible flowers and flourishes in the warm season. The Aizoaceae family features New Zealand spinach, a heat-loving salad green that's not actually spinach but still packs the same nutrients. Another "spinach" comes from the Basellaceae family and is known as Malabar spinach. A climbing plant, Malabar spinach is a nutrient-dense green that thrives in the summer heat.

For cool-season gardening, another plant family called Polygonaceae includes sorrel, with its tangy, citrusy leaves.

Setup

SPACE

When it comes to spacing plants, salad greens might be the most forgiving of all in the garden. If you give them a foot, they'll grow to be a huge lettuce plant. If you give them an inch, they'll grow as

SALAD GREENS GROWING NEEDS BY SIZE

SIZE	SMALL	MEDIUM	LARGE
TYPE	Aster family: spring mix, buttercrunch Amaranth family: spinach Brassica family: arugula	Aster family: romaine, Bibb lettuce Amaranth family: beet greens, larger spinach varieties Brassica family: smaller mustard and kale varieties, bok choy	Aster family: iceberg Amaranth family: Swiss chard Brassica family: kale, mustard, cabbage
SPACING	9–16 plants per square foot	5–9 plants per square foot	1–4 plants per square foot
PLANTING	Directly by seed once the soil can be worked	Directly by seed and/or transplant once the soil can be worked	Start indoors; transplant once the soil can be worked
DAYS TO HARVEST	30–45	45–60	60–90

much as they're able within that little patch of earth.

In a sense, lettuce leaves it up to you. (Get it?)

The space you should allot to salad greens really depends on (a) the output you're hoping to achieve and (b) whether you'd like to cut a couple of leaves from each plant at a time or harvest an entire head of greens at once.

If you're aiming for small leaf harvests, plant the seeds closer together, with as many as 9 to 12 seeds per square foot for smaller greens or at least 1 to 4 seeds per square foot for larger ones. Leafy greens that produce lots of small, harvestable

leaves, even when given minimal space, include spring mixes, buttercrunch, and endive in the aster family; arugula and radish greens in the brassica family; and spinach and beet greens in the amaranth family. Each of these can thrive with only a few square inches in which to grow, and many of them taste best when harvested at 3 to 4 inches in length. Be aware that tight spacing assumes you'll be harvesting often.

If you'd prefer to harvest larger leaves or an entire head of cabbage or romaine at a time, give plants more space to reach maturity. Larger plants include romaine, iceberg lettuces, and radicchio in the aster family; kale, mustards, and cabbages in the brassica family; and Swiss chard in the amaranth family. Though all can actually be grown for baby greens, if left in the garden for longer than 45 to 60 days, these plants will grow leaves that are at least 10 to 12 inches long, with the plants themselves extending as wide as 1 square foot each. So plant these larger plants as many as 4 per square foot or as little as 1 per square foot.

Some greens are best planted by seed directly in garden soil. This is true for soft leafy greens. Their root systems are shallow, which makes it challenging to transplant them without shocking the plant and hindering their growth.

Most leafy greens seeds, from spinach to spring mix to arugula, don't need to be planted deeply. They're very small, and they enjoy a bit of sunlight as they germinate. All you need to do is measure out the seed-planting distance, place the seeds on the surface of the soil, and barely cover the seeds with a bit of compost.

Larger plants, especially those that will grow for months, are ideally started in advance indoors or purchased as transplants. This includes cabbage, mustard, and kale in the brassica family; Swiss chard in the amaranth family; and iceberg and romaine in the aster family. Start these in a mix of coconut coir and compost or organic seed-starting mix indoors under grow lights, and then transplant to the garden at 1 to 4 plants per square foot.

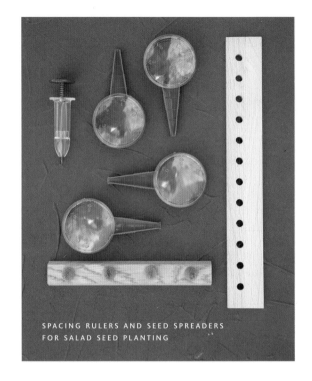

SPACING RULERS AND SEED SPREADERS FOR SALAD SEED PLANTING

SUNLIGHT

As gardeners with close neighbors, my husband and I have done our share of hunting for more sunlight to shine on our garden every place we've lived. You might even say we've been a little desperate to find it.

Jason jumped a fence in Nashville to chop down some wild trees so we could receive a few extra hours of sunlight on our first garden. (Don't worry; no one lived on the other side of the fence.) We shook our heads in disappointment in Houston when we realized that our garden would be in the shadow of our neighbor's oak tree all winter. (Don't worry; we didn't cut that one down.) And in Chicago, our neighbor's home just to the south of us blocked summer sunlight from reaching our kitchen garden in the cooler months of the year.

Unless you're growing in an empty lot or on a treeless prairie, chances are you're fighting for sunlight in your own garden space too. The good news is you don't have to struggle nearly as much when you're growing on Step 3. In fact, it's because of our frustrations with too much shade that I learned the resilience of salad greens.

When the gardening books say, "Find a spot that receives 8 hours of sunlight," they're speaking in ideals and also assuming you'll be growing *all* sorts

The Step-by-Step to Planting Lettuce Seeds

1 Gather lettuce seeds, a seed spacer, and a watering can near a small raised bed.

2 Place the seed spacer along one row.

3 Plant one seed per hole, spacing seeds 1, 2, or 3 inches apart.

4 Use the spacer to press the seeds into the soil.

5 Water in lightly.

6 Cover with hoops and mesh.

of vegetables in that space, including fruiting plants like tomatoes and cucumbers. Too many would-be gardeners call it quits when they hear this instruction and assume their yard doesn't have enough light for any kind of productive gardening.

They're not entirely wrong—sunlight is the central ingredient for a successful garden—but just because your yard isn't basking in 8 or more hours of direct sun doesn't mean you have to close the book on your garden journey. A kitchen garden can still work for you, thanks to leafy greens.

With just 4 hours of sunlight a day, leafy greens produce roots and their first set of leaves, and most lettuce plants will grow to their full potential while receiving less than 5 or 6 hours of sun a day.

It may be true that more hours of sunlight at the right time of year with the right temperatures will give you more leaves, bigger plants, and more production. But you'll find that if you plant enough, you can gather plenty of salad greens from a bed that receives just a few hours of light daily.

So leave the fight for more sun for your fruiting plants (more on that in Steps 6 and 7). For now, find a spot that receives at least 4 hours of sunlight a day, plant your greens there, and fill one harvest basket after another with delicious salad greens, even if you're standing in the shade with your scissors.

For the most part, salad plants thrive in the cooler temperatures of the year. In fact, ideal growing temps for the three key plant families (aster, brassica, and amaranth) range from 45 to 75°F, meaning salad greens grow best in spring and fall or even in winter for some gardeners.

That's not to say that these greens only grow in the cool season. With a little help from you, they can continue through cold and heat.

In cold weather, greens grown under the cover of frost cloth for protection from light frost will hold up until temperatures dip below 25°F. If you really want your greens to push through winter,

Malabar spinach is a salad green that can withstand the heat.

you can grow them under glass, under a small cloche, in a cold frame, or inside a greenhouse, where most greens stay alive and are harvestable even when outside temperatures sink as low as the teens.

In hot weather, you can extend the life of your cool weather–loving salad plants by keeping their roots well watered each day and by covering the plants with shade cloth or a wicker cloche. Providing shade can delay bolting (going to flower and seed) by at least a few weeks and possibly the whole season.

Of course, the best way to push into either the coldest or the hottest parts of the year with salad greens is to grow the varieties that are more tolerant or resistant to the temperature swings. For extreme cold, grow greens with a savoy (bumpy) texture. Brassicas like kale and especially cabbage have savoy varieties.

To push into the hotter months, grow greens that love the heat, such as Malabar spinach, New Zealand spinach, nasturtiums, and mustards.

One final way to extend your salad-garden seasons is by focusing on biennial plants, such as kale and collards from the brassica family and Swiss chard from the amaranth family. These plants don't produce seed until their second full growing year. Biennial plants *need* to survive as long as possible so they make it to their seed-producing year, which means they'll work hard to keep growing through the hottest days. Planting biennials means more greens for you, possibly year-round.

Care

One of my favorite concepts in the garden is "Think about nature."

Because gardening adventures so often begin at the big-box store these days, it's easy to forget that nature has all the answers we need when it comes to plant care and growth.

Anytime I feel confused, frustrated, or downright overwhelmed in the garden, I come back to this question: "How does this grow in nature?" The answer is almost always the solution I'm looking for and the logic I need to keep me growing.

Our kitchen gardens may be made with our own hands, but the main goal is to imitate what happens in the wild. Our best work as gardeners is simply imitating nature as closely as possible.

Consider the life cycle of a buttercrunch plant. After growing lots of leaves, it finally produces a bolted stalk with flowers that bloom. Those flowers dry, each one containing hundreds of tiny seeds, and with the first big rainstorm of autumn, all those seeds drop to the ground. The plant's withered leaves and stalk crumble under the weight of the first snow and freeze in place over the dark months of winter. As the days lengthen in early spring, sunlight hits the soil once more, and the snow begins to melt. Each day another layer of snow turns to water until all we see is dark, wet earth.

What we can't see are the lettuce seeds, the ones that fell onto the soil, where they continue their long winter nap. Day after day the seeds absorb the sun's warmth, the light overhead, and the rain and snowmelt. Finally, full to the brim of cool water in warm soil, the tiny seeds burst right open.

It's easy to assume the first green sprout came up because of the sunshine. Yes, light was definitely part of the equation. However, the thing that was most consistent for those seeds was water. That slow snowmelt provided consistent moisture for the seeds until they simply had to burst open and sprout.

And that's the picture to keep in mind when you're watering your lettuce greens.

Most lettuce plants are 90 to 95 percent water. To successfully grow lettuce

the soil dry out one bit before the seeds show their first signs of green.

Once the seeds are established, continue to keep the plants well watered. Lettuce plants have shallow roots that grow right under the soil's surface, putting them at risk of drying out sooner than more deeply planted seeds. So water lettuce seedlings consistently, maintaining a moist soil environment and being certain the water hits the roots of the plants, not the leaves.

As lettuce plants grow, their leaves will tell you when to water and when to pause. If leaves begin to wilt, that's a sign you should have watered about 2 days ago; you'll have to baby the greens back to life over the next few days. If leaves turn yellow, you've watered too much. And if leaves show signs of mold or mildew or the stem starts to rot, you're watering way too much.

Let nature be your guide when it comes to watering your salad plants: remember that slow snowmelt; give them a little water, not too much; and keep it consistent. Follow these rules and you're 98 percent of the way there.

NUTRIENTS

The good news about growing salad greens is that they must only reach the third stage of their maturity before we harvest and enjoy them. That's because leaves are the only thing we want from these plants.

greens, watering must be your major focus. More important than the amount of water is the frequency of watering. So there's one word to remember when it comes to your salad greens watering plan: *consistency*.

If you're growing lettuce greens, you've now got a new habit to add to your gardening routine, and that's checking the moisture level of your salad plants.

The most crucial time for consistent watering is before the seeds germinate. Think about nature here and do your best imitation of melting snow. Don't let

This means less work for you, plus faster harvests.

And if you set up your leafy green plants to grow in rich, compost-amended soil, they won't require additional fertilizing. Compost-rich soil provides the key nutrients—namely nitrogen and magnesium—salad greens need to thrive.

That said, if you would like to boost leafy green production, encouraging the plants to grow bigger and perhaps faster, or if the leaves lose their bright green hue, you can fertilize every 2 to 4 weeks to add a bit of nitrogen to the plant's system. Be careful to think of nature and use only organic ingredients like cotton-seed meal, earthworm castings, or extra compost as the source of nitrogen; if you use a synthetically derived fertilizer, you risk burning the leaves.

NUTRIENT NEEDS OF SALAD GREENS

LEAF CHANGE	LEAF STAGE	NUTRIENT ISSUE	RECOMMENDED AMENDMENT
Yellowed leaves	Old growth	Nitrogen deficiency	Add cottonseed meal
Yellow-edged leaves	Old growth	Magnesium deficiency	Add compost, Epsom salts, or magnesium
Warped, misshapen new leaves	New growth	Calcium deficiency	Add gypsum, lime, or hardwood ashes
Purple or reddish leaves	New growth	Phosphorus deficiency	Add bat guano, bone meal, or rock phosphate

Listen to your plants; they'll tell you when they need a little something extra. See page 105 for a guide to interpreting your leafy greens' language.

TENDING

"*Ugh*, the caterpillars!"

It was my third year growing salad greens (so I obviously knew everything on the subject), and I had just conceived a plan to sell homegrown salad greens to my neighbors.

I told a few local businesses and neighbors that I'd be delivering just-harvested lettuce leaves from my garden every day for lunch. Jason offered his muscle to support my garden business dreams, and we turned three 1-foot-tall garden beds into six 6-inch-tall garden beds. I promptly covered them all with lettuce seeds.

As expected, within about 30 days, I started to harvest the first leafy greens from my new boxes, and I did a test run of washing, sorting, and packaging the greens before I was ready to sell.

But what I found in the kitchen sink was something no one would buy: a bunch of wriggly caterpillars. These were cabbage loopers, little green critters that munch on leaves at will in their early caterpillar stages, form chrysalises, and then emerge as white moths, each female capable of laying hundreds of new caterpillar eggs in a matter of days.

The fact that I was discovering caterpillars at this stage could only mean that there were likely hundreds more in my future product. *Ugh* was the best thing I could think to say. I knew I could treat the caterpillars organically, but I immediately regretted not protecting my salad plants in the first place.

They say "an ounce of prevention is worth a pound of cure," but you'll actually need a few yards for pest protection in the salad garden. Yards of tulle or garden mesh, that is.

Take it from me and my caterpillar-infested garden: put most of your tending efforts into protecting your greens from pests and disease rather than treating the problems once they arise.

The best way to do this in the salad garden is with covers. Tulle or mesh fabric offers the perfect protection for salad greens. The tiny holes in the fabric are big enough to allow sunlight, water, and air to reach the plants yet small enough to keep out moths, slugs, beetles,

and then reapply and secure the cover again until next time.

If (I mean *when*) pests do arrive on salad garden plants, there are ways you can treat them organically. The first measure is to remove all damaged leaves—be ruthless!—and clean the soil around the plant. Over the next 2 weeks, continue plucking off damaged leaves and picking up dead plant material and weeds from the soil.

If severe cutting and cleaning don't rid the plants of the pest, you can apply a spray or granular treatment. My favorites for the salad garden are garlic barrier (an extract of garlic mixed with water and sprayed on plants) or diluted castile soap. In extreme pest infestations, you could use Monterey B.t., but if the pest issue is that severe, I typically just remove the affected plants, clean the area, and start again.

Beyond protecting the garden, your most important tending task is harvesting continuously.

By harvesting lettuce greens, you're actually tending them. When you remove the oldest and lowest leaves from each plant, you make sure the soil is clear of leaf debris and encourage new growth from the center of each plant. Just as in Step 2, tending and harvesting are pretty much the same thing. If that's not a gardener's win, I don't know what is.

Beyond harvesting to eat, regularly cut the older and outer leaves from the plants, even if they don't look fit for consumption because of holes, spots,

leafhoppers, and caterpillars. Simply covering greens with hoops and a piece of agricultural mesh fabric or tulle can prevent all kinds of critters from entering your bed, saving all the beautiful greens for *you* to enjoy—not the pests!

Protecting your leafy greens will spare you a lot of grief, but you've got to time it right. As soon as you plant the seeds or starter plants outside, cover them. Waiting a few days or weeks, especially after the first leaves appear, can mean you'll end up trapping the pests *inside* the garden instead of keeping them out.

Once your greens are protected with a cover, you simply lift the mesh when you need to tend or harvest the plants,

Work with Nature

Salad greens play well with other plants in the garden, and plants will stay healthier when you work with nature. Plant chives, green onions, garlic, and onions around your greens as a natural pest deterrent (pests smell the onions and not the leafy greens). Grow edible flowers such as calendulas and nasturtiums as "trap crops"—plants that attract pests to their flowers and scent, enticing the pests away from the salad greens.

Grow herbs in the Apiaceae family near salad greens to welcome beneficial insects like ladybugs to the salad garden. These insects prey on lettuce's predators (like aphids) and will work alongside you to keep your lettuce for you, not the bugs.

Finally, plant greens alongside "nitrogen-fixing" fruit plants like peas and beans that absorb nitrogen from soil bacteria and can share that growth-spurring nitrogen with salad greens so they grow strong. You can also plant salad greens in the shade of taller fruiting plants like tomatoes or cucumbers to keep the greens cool when temperatures warm up.

or other damage. Generally, I toss these leaves into the compost pile, but if there are signs of disease, I'll put them in a separate space for green waste.

Those caterpillars might have gnawed their way through my first business idea, but they ultimately taught me important lessons in tending my salad garden. A little mesh and regular harvesting go a long way.

Harvest

TIME

Though the wait to harvest salad leaves is longer than that for sprouts and microgreens, I'd still classify lettuces as garden "fast food." Baby greens like radish leaves and arugula are ready to harvest in less than 30 days, and most other salad greens will be ready to cut after 45 days. That's under 6 weekends between your planting day and first harvest day.

Once you hold a lettuce, kale, or arugula seed in your hand, you won't be able to look at a head of lettuce or plastic tub of arugula the same way again.

"All this can come from just *that* in such a short time?"

It's an everyday miracle that most of us take for granted when browsing the grocery store refrigerated section. But not you. Not after you complete your first few weeks of salad gardening. From now on, romaine is remarkable, kale

TROUBLESHOOTING PESTS AND DISEASES OF SALAD GREENS

PESTS/ DISEASE	SIGN OF PROBLEM	PREVENTION	INITIAL TREATMENT	SECOND TREATMENT
Aphids	Misshapen, curling, stunted, or yellowing leaves	Check plants early, don't overfertilize, plant near onions	Apply insecticidal soap or dust plants with flour	Apply neem oil
Cabbage looper	Holes on inside of leaves, dark and small balls on leaves	Use mesh or tulle cover	Cut away damaged leaves, clean soil area, search for caterpillars in soil, keep watch, and repeat this process every few days	Spray leaves with castile soap or garlic barrier
Mold or mildew	White cottony growth, lighter green to yellow spots near the veins of leaves	Don't overwater, maintain airflow between plants	Prune back affected leaves, clean soil area, thin plants to increase airflow	Apply insecticidal soap or organic fungicide
Slugs, snails	Holes in leaf edges and centers, nearby slime trails, chewed-off seedlings with nothing but midribs left	Create a barrier to the plant with copper tape, sprinkle diatomaceous earth around plants	Remove damaged leaves from soil area, clean bottom of plant, add fresh finished compost	Sprinkle organic Sluggo around base of plants

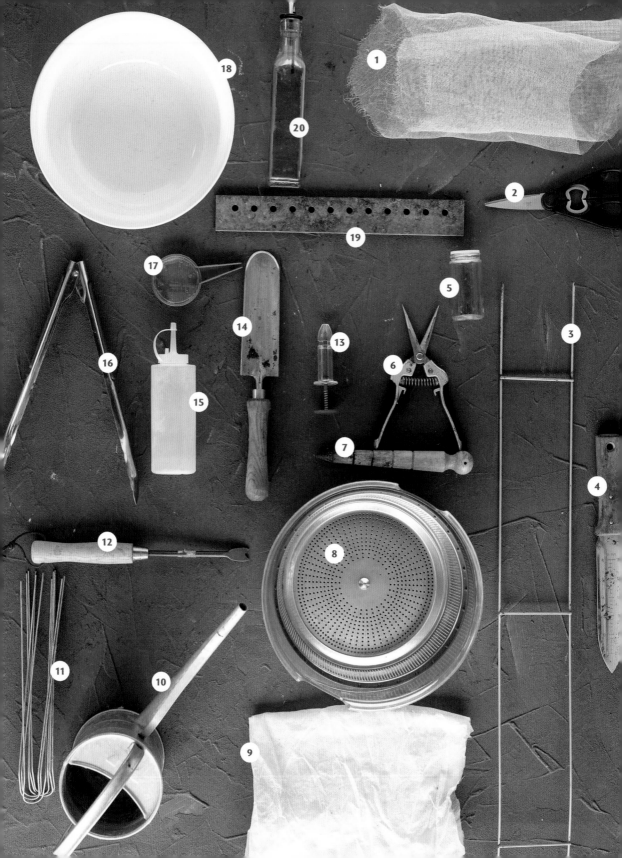

1 GARDEN MESH	10 WATERING CAN
2 HARVEST SCISSORS	11 U PINS
3 HOOPS FOR GARDEN MESH AND FROST CLOTH	12 WEEDER
	13 SEED INJECTOR
4 HORI HORI KNIFE	14 GARDEN TROVEL
5 SPICE JAR FOR SEED SPREADING	15 SEED DISTRIBUTOR
	16 SALAD TONGS
6 NEEDLE-NOSE PRUNERS	17 SEED SPREADER
	18 HARVEST BOWL
7 DIBBER	19 SEED SPACER
8 SALAD SPINNER	20 GARDEN SALAD DRESSING CONTAINER
9 FROST CLOTH	

is unbelievable, and, yes, even spinach is a wonder.

As soon as you plant your lettuce seeds, mark your calendar 45 days forward with a star that reads: "First harvest of the best salad I've ever tasted in my life."

PRODUCTION

As soon as our first salad gardens started growing, my family couldn't shove the greens in our mouths fast enough. So I did what any smart mother who desperately needs help from friends and neighbors would do: I shared the bounty.

Actually, it was these garden barters that first got me thinking about starting a gardening business. (This was before I spotted the caterpillars . . .)

You'll see exactly what I mean in terms of full harvest baskets once your lettuce plants begin showing leaves. Follow these

steps and you might just find yourself equipped with new bribing power for puppy walking or kid watching too.

One of the reasons leaves are so much fun to grow is that they grow so much. You can get pounds of lettuce from just one plant in a very short period of time. In fact, I expect to get at least one full salad bowl per month from each lettuce plant. So if I've planted 9 salad plants in a square foot, I expect to get nine small bowls of lettuce within a 45- to 75-day period from just that one spot.

If I'm growing bigger leaves from head lettuces like cabbage and iceberg, I anticipate one huge harvest that could feed all of us from 1 square foot after 60 days, and if it's a large cut-and-come-again plant like kale, I'll harvest weekly from

Salad Green Focus: Arugula

Arugula, also called "rocket," is a bit of an odd leaf out, in all the best ways. First, it's in the brassica family (among all those super good-for-you dark leafy greens), but it doesn't take up nearly as much space or need as much growing time as most of its cousins. Its soft, easy-to-pick leaves that you can cut from again and again are more like the lettuces you'll find in the aster family.

Arugula is not picky about temperature. It's more heat tolerant than most salad greens, and it can withstand some frost. I grew arugula year-round in Houston; in Chicago, I enjoy at least 8 months of production.

To grow arugula, sow seeds in a sandy loam soil with a high compost content (see page 69). The simplest sowing method is to take a bunch of the tiny seeds in hand and rub your fingers together over the raised bed to scatter the seeds right on top of the soil. Use your hand to rough up the soil a bit afterward. You don't want to bury arugula seeds deeply—they just need to make soil contact. Plants will grow close together, so you should commit to harvesting the leaves when they're smaller. Otherwise, you'll need to take time to separate the seeds and stagger your rows.

Water your seeds in well, and seedlings will emerge in 6 to 10 days. Baby greens will be ready in 3 to 4 weeks, and a full-size plant will grow in about 6 weeks. Personally, I prefer the leaves when they're smaller. (If you don't like the taste of store-bought varieties, you've *got* to try freshly cut baby arugula.)

You can harvest arugula in one of two ways. The first is by using needle-nose pruners to cut one leaf stem at a time, right at the base of the plant. Take only the outer leaves and preserve the younger leaves so they can continue to grow. The second (and faster) way to harvest is what I officially call the "ponytail-chop method." Grab a bunch of leaves in your hand like you're gathering hair for a ponytail and cut all the leaves at once at the base, leaving only 1 to 2 inches of greens at the bottom to keep producing.

You might be surprised how much arugula you can harvest from a couple of plants. Throw your leaves in pasta or soup, eat them fresh, make a pesto, or braise them.

that 1 square foot of space for at least 3 to 6 months (if not longer).

It's good to think forward to harvest time when planning and planting your salad greens. Before sowing any seeds, estimate the number of greens servings you'd love to have for your household per month. Remember, this isn't just for raw salad. I use greens in morning smoothies, in dips and side dishes, in stir-fries and sautéed meals too.

I usually estimate a little under two servings a day for myself and my husband and one serving every few days for each of my kids (one can hope!). This adds up to about 150 greens servings per month for our household. When I divide those servings by 4 or 5 plants per square foot, I know I need at least 30 square feet of salad plants growing intensively to keep the harvests coming.

Once your plants get started, it can be hard to keep up with everything that's coming out of the garden. Harvest one leaf, and another one is already growing to replace it. The majority of plants from the aster family and some from the brassica and amaranth families will produce new and delicious leaves for 60 to 90 days if the temperatures stay below 80°F. When temps rise higher, it will be time to either let these plants bolt and produce seed (see Step 8) or simply remove them from the garden altogether.

Biennial plants like Swiss chard and kale provide new leaves and servings for months to come. As soon as you pull the cool-season greens, you can plant some warm-season greens to give you harvests instead. They'll provide another 45 to 75 days of harvest before it's time to return to cool-season greens once more.

If you have a hot season in your climate, fill in with heat-tolerant greens like Malabar spinach, sorrel, and longevity spinach too.

Taking This Step

Once you take this step, you'll soon enjoy the most delicious salad greens you've ever tasted. They don't just taste good; they *are* so good for you. These freshly harvested leaves contain more nutrition than any salad green you can purchase.

And they're not just good for you; they're good for the planet too. With every bite of homegrown salad, you're cutting down on food miles and single-use plastics—and let's not forget the food waste you're avoiding. In between salads and green smoothies, your greens aren't turning slimy in the fridge. They're still growing in your garden—staying healthy and fresh until you're ready to consume another harvest. Instead of facing spoiled plastic boxes of lettuce, you're spoiling yourself with salad you actually like to eat.

Consider yourself warned: once you've tasted homegrown greens, it will be hard to go back to the grocery variety. Don't be mad at me if it's garden greens for you or none at all after you take this step.

Surprisingly Edible Leaves

Eating the leaves of certain plants is unconventional. But even tomatoes, peppers, beans, cucumbers, and okra plants have leaves that are edible (although you may not care for the taste or texture). Note: Whenever you try any new plant food, always eat a small amount to start. Not all foods agree with all people, and some can irritate or be toxic in large amounts.

Growing 6 Months
of Salad Greens

SET UP

- Select a site with 4+ hours of sunlight.
- Prepare a raised bed or container (minimum of 6 inches tall).
- Add sandy loam soil (see page 69).
- Provide a consistent water source with drip irrigation or a regular hand-watering schedule.
- Plant in cool-season temps (35 to 65°F) or in the warm season (for heat-tolerant greens).

PLANT

- Plant by seed or carefully transplant small plants.
- Keep well watered until germination.

TEND

- Cover with mesh or tulle.
- Add nutrients when needed.
- Water consistently.

HARVEST

- Cut the outer and lower leaves often.
- Harvest weekly after 45 days.
- Remove the plant once it bolts (produces flowers and seeds).

part three **roots**

If you were the kid who always begged your friends to play one more round of hide-and-seek, or you've been hoping someone will throw you a surprise party one day, then growing roots, bulbs, tubers, and rhizomes might just be your new favorite thing in the garden because—*surprise!*—there's always something hidden, waiting for you to find it.

For many of us, the garden is all about what meets the eye: green leaves, glossy fruit, colorful flowers.

But when the thing you want to harvest grows underground, you've got to enjoy the hunt and accept the fact that most of the magic will happen out of sight and after you close your eyes and count to 100.

Whenever I share the LRF system, explaining how graduating from leaves to roots to fruit is the way to mature as a kitchen gardener, someone interrupts and insists that it was easier for them to grow fruiting crops than to grow roots. And that may be true for them. But I think it's the unknown factor, the *Is anything even happening down there?* aspect, that makes growing roots feel more difficult to some gardeners, not the plants' demands.

So when I say that growing roots is the next step in the kitchen garden, keep in mind that this step does come with its own set of challenges. But roots really are just a little more demanding than salad greens in terms of their sunlight, space, time, and tending needs. Even though what's going on beneath the surface of the soil can be a mystery, what your root plants require to grow and thrive is not.

Think of roots as storage units for plants. They hold most of the nutrients these plants need as they grow and mature. When a plant gets extra nutrients, water, or sunshine, it sends down deposits to the roots to save for the future.

When storms hit, intense winds blow, or temperatures change, plants strengthen their roots. In fact, plants

grown in static conditions often need to be "roughed up" or shaken artificially to imitate wind and typical weather patterns that stimulate new growth in roots. Healthy roots are a sign that a plant has been through some things and knows how to stay alive despite it.

As you grow roots, consider the fact that you're growing food stores, suitcases full of nutrients that you'll bring into your own storehouse—i.e., your kitchen. The bottom parts of plants are built for endurance and longevity, which means your root harvests will last longer on the shelf or in the fridge than their leafy counterparts. (This is why you often see radish or beet roots at the grocery store but not radish or beet leaves, though the leaves are just as edible.)

These roots won't just last longer; they'll retain their nutrients for more days after harvest too. Since roots are designed for long-term nutrition storage for the plant itself, carrots, beets, celeriac, parsnips, and radishes maintain their vitamin content after harvest much better than leafy greens. In fact, these are some of the most nutritious foods you can bite into.

Because nutrition is such a big part of a root's function, you'll need to pay closer attention to the makeup of your soil by testing it before planting, adding important nutrients like phosphorus and potassium before digging in, and checking soil levels throughout the growing season.

KNOW YOUR BULBS, RHIZOMES, ROOTS, AND TUBERS

PLANT	ROOT, TUBER, OR BULB?	SPACING	PLANTING METHOD	SEASON
Beet (Amaranthaceae family)	Root	6–9 per square foot	By seed	Cool
Carrot (Apiaceae family)	Root	16 per square foot	By seed	Cool
Garlic (Amaryllidaceae family)	Bulb	9 per square foot	By clove	Cool
Ginger (Zingiberaceae family)	Rhizome	1 per 2–3 square feet	By rhizome cutting	Warm to hot
Onion (Amaryllidaceae family)	Bulb	9 per square foot	By seed or set	Cool to warm
Potato (Solanaceae family)	Tuber	1 per square foot	By cut tuber	Warm
Radish (Brassicaceae family)	Root	36 per square foot	By seed	Cool
Rutabaga (Brassicaceae family)	Root	6–9 per square foot	By seed	Cool
Sweet potato (Convolvulaceae family)	Tuber	1 per square foot	By slip	Hot
Turmeric (Zingiberaceae family)	Rhizome	1 per 2–3 square feet	By rhizome cutting	Warm or hot
Turnip (Brassicaceae family)	Root	6–9 per square foot	By seed	Cool

But before we get too far into the mechanics of growing roots, let's get clear on what's called a "root" and what's not. I can't have you reading this book and telling your friends you're growing roots when you're actually growing tubers. We have a reputation to uphold as kitchen gardeners, right? So let's be sure you know the distinctions between roots, tubers, bulbs, and rhizomes. Having some clarity here matters not only so you don't get corrected by the plant police but so you can grow each plant the way it prefers.

You may be surprised (like I was) to learn that a potato is not actually called a "root."

Neither are onions or garlic.

But they all grow underground . . . Isn't that the definition of a root?

A root is an organ that typically forms underground to anchor the plant in place, store food, and absorb water and other nutrients from the soil. Plants that are considered root crops with a centralized taproot include radishes, beets, carrots, parsnips, fennel, and celeriac.

A tuber, like a root, can store nutrients for the plant, but it's also capable of growing into a new plant through its buds. Potatoes and sweet potatoes are tubers.

A bulb isn't a root but a modified stem that contains an underground bud with overlapping leaves. Garlic, onion, and leeks are all technically bulbs.

A rhizome is the main stem of the plant that grows horizontally underground. While you might call it "ginger-root," ginger technically comes from a rhizome, as does turmeric.

There are underground crops to grow for every garden season. In the cold months, carrots will grow slowly under frost cloth or a cold frame, as long as they were planted before frost and snow arrived. You might also have garlic and possibly onions growing or at least settling in during the coldest part of the year. In the cool season, you can plant radishes, carrots, beets, onions, and garlic. In the warm season, you can grow potatoes. In the heat of summer, you can grow sweet potatoes, ginger, and turmeric.

If you take advantage of your growing seasons, your garden can be a bed of surprises year-round. The next two steps will remove some of the mystery (but none of the fun) around growing roots, tubers, bulbs, and rhizomes.

STEP 4

Roots

"We pulled all the carrots, Mommy," Rebekah yelled to me in passing. As if it was no big thing.

I was in the kitchen (as usual) and immediately felt a sense of dread. "*All the carrots?*" I asked.

"All" meant an entire 4-by-10-foot garden bed planted with nothing but carrots. That's 40 square feet of garden space, if you're counting, and if you plant like I do, that's at least 400 carrots.

"Yep. Don't worry. We washed them off in our bathroom."

Four hundred carrots hauled through the living room and washed by a pre-schooler in the bathroom sink? This was testing me.

But it wasn't the dirt-clogged sink that was the issue. I was just jealous they'd pulled all those carrots while I was stuck in the kitchen. If you've never pulled a carrot you grew yourself, you don't know it yet, but a carrot harvest is not something you'd want to miss.

Let me fill you in:

When you give a gentle pull on the stem, you'll feel the resistance from the earth below. You pull some more and can almost sense that it's you and the garden in a tug-of-war. She's not going to give up easily.

Your garden soil has allowed this root to swell and expand over the past few months. This root has literally moved its own mountains—pushing soil ten times its weight out of its way, all while absorbing the water and the air and the nutrients that surround it.

When you finally win (and you will), your eyes widen and your heart might even skip a beat at the first peek of the root top—its color, its width, its stretch marks. The stem is now a magical thread you can't help but keep pulling. You desperately want to see the end, but at the same time, you pull as slowly as you can to enjoy the experience as long as possible. Finally—*pop!* The full carrot appears.

You turn your little root on its side and admire it—bumps, stretch marks, dirt, and all. Never has a plant meant so much. From now on, you're hooked. You look down, search the garden for another stem that looks ready to pull, and start the experience all over again.

It was this "pop" that kept my girls quietly occupied all that time in the garden, and I'd missed the whole thing.

Yes, there would be a mess, and yes, there would be a lot of carrot soufflé, juice, and cake in our very near future. But more than anything, I'd missed the carrot-picking show. So somewhere between cleaning the bathroom and cooking the carrots, I'd just have to get out there and plant more seeds.

This step in your gardener's journey is a big one. You're going from loads of leaves aboveground to hidden treasures below. Instead of knowing exactly what your harvest will look like from day to day, you'll have dozens of days when you can only guess what's growing underneath the surface.

This step is more challenging but can also be so rewarding, especially if you get to the harvest before your preschooler does.

Plant Families

You'll grow three key plant families of root crops in the garden. If you've just completed Step 3, then the families will sound familiar. There's overlap between the plant families you'll encounter on each step, and it's fun to think that we can grow some of these plants for their leaves, some for their roots, and some for both.

Apiaceae. This family houses herbs like cilantro and dill. It's best known for the carrot root crop, but it also includes fennel, parsnip, and the less-well-known

FAMILY	COMMON PLANTS
Amaranthaceae	Beets
Apiaceae	Carrot, celeriac, fennel, parsnip
Brassicaceae	Radish, turnip, rutabaga

but super nutritious root celeriac. These plants prefer the cool season and grow best in deep raised beds that make room for their taproots to grow as long and deep as possible.

Brassicaceae. The brassica family is usually thought of in terms of leafy greens like kale and mustards, but it also includes roots like radishes, turnips, and rutabaga. These plants also love the cool season and grow bulbous roots quickly underground as their leaves grow tall and wide above.

Amaranthaceae. The amaranth family, known best for spinach, includes beetroots too. Amaranth plants prefer the cool season and need adequate space for the full root to form.

There are other plant families you can grow for their roots, but these are the most common and the best to focus on as you move through this step.

As you plant the different families in this step, always be thinking of the roots. "Out of sight, out of mind" is a thing. In other words, it's easy to focus mostly on what's growing aboveground even when

you're gearing up to grow root plants. So the key here is: just because you can't see it doesn't mean it's not there.

Setup

SPACE

Have you heard of the "pot-size effect"? It's the idea that a plant will grow to the size of its pot and no further. It's based on scientific discoveries that plants extend roots to the edges of their

container to get a sense of how big they can grow, and that all plant species reach larger sizes when grown in a bigger pot.

The pot-size effect is something to consider when you set up root plants. Picture the tiny seeds of your future root crop. Day after day, each seed develops a root that grows and swells and adds new cells. That is, until the root detects something big nearby: another plant. Even though your root crops will likely be grown in a raised bed or at least a large container, imagine each plant as being in its own invisible pot. If you plant root

The Step-by-Step to Planting Radish Seeds

1 Gather a dibber, seeds, and a watering can near the kitchen garden.

2 Make straight lines with the dibber at least 3 inches apart.

3 Use the dibber to mark holes at ½-inch depth spaced 1 inch apart.

4 Place one seed in each hole.

5 Use the flat side of the dibber to settle the seeds.

6 Water in carefully (1 inch per week).

seeds too close together, you've given each plant a small container that will prevent it from growing to its full potential.

So keep in mind the pot-size effect and the desired harvest size of the mature radish, carrot, beet, or even celeriac when determining how much space to give each root plant seed you put in the garden.

If you're growing radishes that are 2 inches wide when mature, you can plant 36 in 1 square foot. If you're growing carrots that are 3 inches wide, you can plant 16 carrots in 1 square foot. If you're growing beets that are 4 inches wide, you can plant 9 beets per square foot.

Imagining how large each plant can become is easier said than done. Most root crop seeds, especially radishes, carrots, and beets, are tiny. Simply separating the pebble-like seeds can be difficult on its own, but holding each seed in its place and being sure each one is planted apart from another is next-level gardening.

When it comes to spacing, get it right the first time. In other words, don't assume you'll have time to return to the garden to thin your seedlings once they sprout. Slowing down to space out your seeds correctly from the beginning will save you days and seasons of frustration because you won't have to thin and separate seedlings planted too closely together.

It's easy to be lazy with your planting and just toss out a bunch of seeds all at once. (Trust me, I know.) But I've found that managing and thinning closely planted seeds takes way more time than simply slowing down in the beginning and planting methodically.

SUNLIGHT

Roots are in between leaves and fruit in terms of their sunlight needs. You'll still see a lot of growth on your plants without the ideal amount of sunlight, but that growth will mostly be *above* the soil instead of below, where we want it most. In general, 6 hours of direct sunlight on your root plants is necessary for good, strong root formation under the soil.

Because root crops are usually smaller plants with greens that don't grow very high above the ground, you'll need to carefully choose their planting location so that larger-fruiting plants (and even larger-leafed plants like kales and herbs) don't block the sun from the root crops.

When I first began gardening, I read that radishes and carrots grew well together, but I've found the opposite to be true. The leaves of the radishes are so large and thick that they shade the carrots too early in their growth. While I did end up getting a radish harvest, the carrots never recovered from their days under the radishes' shadow. Now I know to plant each of them separately in their own bed or to space them apart in the garden, so they don't miss a day of the sunshine they need for speedy growth.

Root plants can take longer to germinate and grow than leafy greens. I find that roots do best when planted by themselves in a garden bed instead of alongside leafy greens and fruiting plants. Yes, you can still use the intensive planting guide from my first book, *Kitchen Garden Revival*, to grow root crops alongside other types of plants. But start your root crops in the garden *first* so their leaves have enough time to grow 4 to 6 inches before the leafy greens or fruiting plants around them take off and take up their space.

SEASON

Most of the plants we enjoy most for their roots are planted in the cool season when temperatures range from 45 to 75°F. Any colder, and root crops won't germinate; any warmer, and most will stall their growth or never fully form a root.

Most roots love it when the days are warm, not hot, and the nights are cool, not cold. This means you'll get the best harvests from root crops during the "shoulder" seasons of spring and fall, or whatever time of year is equivalent to a cool season in your neighborhood. When I gardened in Houston, I planted root crops in winter, but in the Chicago area, I grow them twice a year—in spring and fall.

The timing can be tricky. You need the soil warm enough to be able to sow the seeds, but if you plant too late (once temperatures are already rising and your cool season is transitioning to warm), your crops will bolt and go to seed before they fully develop great roots.

And if you wait too late at the end of the warm season to plant, the soil and air temperatures will become too cold before the roots can fully form.

The trick is to look for weather that will be over 45°F but below 85°F for 2 to 3 months. If you can find this window as the weather either warms or cools, plant as soon as you can at the beginning of that time frame.

Once you're growing any of the key root crops (carrots, parsnips, and celeriac from the Apiaceae family; radishes, turnips, and rutabagas from the

Brassicaceae family; or beets from the Amaranthaceae family), you'll need to consistently check your soil temperature to keep things between 55 and 75°F for best root formation.

Weather-protection techniques can help regulate soil temperature and extend your growing time. During the transition from cold season to cool season, for example, you could use a frost cloth or cold frame when you first plant. If your seeds need to germinate and begin to grow during the warm season, use a shade cloth to protect the roots and cool the soil. Then, as the seeds sprout and temperatures decrease a bit, you can remove the shade cloth and allow the plants to grow in the open air.

Care

WATER

Because root crops are typically planted by seed, consistent water at the outset of the plant's growth is essential to ensure the seeds make it to the seedling stage. This is particularly true for carrots, beets, radishes, turnips, and parsnips. During germination, seeds need to swell to the point of bursting; to get to that point, they must stay wet for days. While the soil doesn't need to be soaking wet, it should be a little moist to the touch and never dry out completely.

Water root crops, especially the tiny-seed varieties, with care, as heavy watering (and heavy rain) can easily displace the seeds that you've so carefully spaced and sown. The best way to water root seeds and seedlings is from overhead with a gentle spray head that allows the water to evenly disperse over the soil's surface instead of pooling in any one spot.

Once the seeds are established and the greens start to show, root crops still need regular watering. The easiest way to ensure consistent water long-term is to install a drip-irrigation or soaker-hose system that puts the water at root level, where plants need it most, rather than at leaf level. You can set a watering schedule for your root crops for every 2 to 3 days, making sure your plants get at least 1 inch of rain or supplemental water per week.

NUTRIENTS

Unlike the plants we explored in Steps 1 through 3, root crops need extra

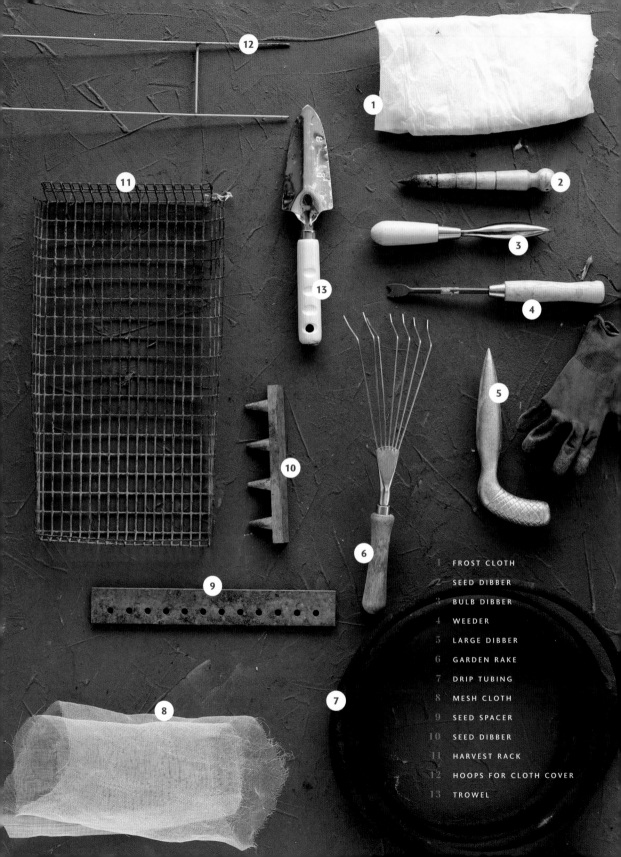

1   FROST CLOTH

2   SEED DIBBER

3   BULB DIBBER

4   WEEDER

5   LARGE DIBBER

6   GARDEN RAKE

7   DRIP TUBING

8   MESH CLOTH

9   SEED SPACER

10   SEED DIBBER

11   HARVEST RACK

12   HOOPS FOR CLOTH COVER

13   TROWEL

nutrients designed to encourage stronger and bigger roots rather than more leaves.

Though nitrogen was important for growth in Steps 1 through 3, it's not the thing to give root crops. In fact, it's a good idea to test your soil before you plant root crops to be sure your soil blend isn't too heavy with nitrogen.

Too much nitrogen means you'll end up with lots of greens on your plants and very small roots. On more than one occasion, I've watched lush, beautiful plants grow above the soil line, only to pull the radishes, carrots, or beets and be thoroughly disappointed by the tiny roots underneath.

So if not nitrogen, what are the two main nutrients that support healthy root growth? Phosphorus and potassium. Dosing your soil with these two nutrients when plants are just beginning to develop will encourage them to form thick new roots and strengthen existing ones, whereas adding these nutrients later in the plants' lives will encourage the formation of flowers and fruit—not the thing you're growing these plants for. To get these nutrients to the root crops when they need it, apply phosphorus and potassium *before* planting the root crops. Work the fertilizer several inches into the soil to put those nutrients right where the developing roots can reach them.

If shopping for root crop fertilizer, look for an N-P-K ratio where the second and third numbers (for phosphorus and potassium, respectively) are higher than the first number (for nitrogen). And I

always recommend natural and organic inputs made from composts or natural waste products.

TENDING

To get the most root growth from your plants during their short growing period, your focus should be on:

1 Maintaining a consistent moisture level

2 Giving the roots as much room to grow as possible by planting methodically and thinning plants regularly

3 Ensuring that the nutrients added contribute to more root growth than leaf growth by using phosphorus and potassium instead of nitrogen-rich fertilizers early in the plants' growth period

take care of themselves, needing you only to check for weeds, monitor water, and harvest.

Again, watering is key in the first few weeks after planting seeds. But once sprouted, your root crops need just an inch of water per week—from your watering system or from the sky—to keep growing.

As a root grows, it first develops a small radicle and then its first set of leaves. These leaves are critical to the growth of the root because they use sunlight to send energy to the root itself. Our goal with growing root crops is for the root itself to swell and grow as large as possible during the optimal growing period.

Once the root crop seedlings begin to sprout, you'll see how well you spaced each seed. Does every plant have the amount of soil and sunlight it needs? I use my fingers to measure between seedlings to determine if they are the right distance apart (two fingers for a radish, three fingers for a carrot, four fingers for a beet, five fingers for celeriac).

If seedlings are crowding each other, it's time to thin. Look for two seedlings too close together and pick one of those to remove, ideally whichever one seems a little more spindly or less hardy than its neighbor.

Thin the root crop seedlings as soon as their true leaves appear. Hesitation in thinning will result in the plant experiencing a prolonged state of stress over whether it will receive the nutrients and

If you're entering a busy season in life when you know you can't commit a lot of time to tending the garden but you're still hoping to have a harvest, growing root crops can be the answer. Once planted, watered in, and thinned, most root crops

A Special Note about Beet Seeds

Each beet seed is actually a seed cluster containing 2 or 3 (or even 5) seeds. These multigerm seeds form when beet flowers grow in clusters fused together by the petals. For every beet seed you plant, you should expect to thin 1, 2, or even 3 seedlings to allow each remaining beet enough room to grow to its fullest potential.

water it needs. So don't wait to thin your crop, or you will delay your plants putting on their best roots possible.

To thin, you can either pull the entire seedling out, root and all, or you can trim the extra seedling at the soil level with a pair of scissors. The second is less likely to damage the root of the remaining plant—plus it's less of a dirty job!

Next, be sure the watering is consistent for your root crops. If carrot seeds or radish seeds dry out during their germination or early growth period, this can slow the growth of their roots by days or even weeks.

Finally, be certain sunshine levels remain as high as possible for your root crop plants as they continue to grow. Days of growing under the shade of a larger plant will stunt and slow their growth, if not end it altogether.

Clearing the soil area around root crops is important to protect your roots from pests. Once a week, gently rake away debris like fallen leaves, spent plants (those that are wilting or dying), or airborne weeds that have begun to take hold. Root crops tend to be sensitive little things—they're constantly aware of their surroundings and will sometimes refuse to grow further if they sense another plant nearby.

When clearing the soil area, if you see part of an underdeveloped root aboveground, simply hill fresh soil around the exposed shoulder up to the beginning of the stem. Hilling is the process of pushing compost or soil up along the main stem of the plant. By hilling soil, you bury the roots a bit deeper so they can more fully develop before harvest.

Harvest

TIME

The challenge with waiting on root crops is not that they are slow in their growth (most will be ready to harvest in 2 months); it's more the uncertainty of when they will be ready.

The plant's greens can hint at what's happening underground. In general, the root's size imitates the growth aboveground.

Even while you're tapping your foot with impatience waiting for your radishes or beets to be ready, there are plenty of greens on those plants that you can pluck and enjoy long before the underground treats.

If you've given your plants adequate space, enough water, the right balance of nutrients in the soil, and all the sunshine available, many of your root crops should be ready for harvest in less than 2 months.

Though you do need to wait patiently for the harvest, it's also important to avoid leaving root crops in the ground for too long. At their peak, these roots will be crunchy and crisp, but as the days wear on, they can grow tough and develop side roots. There is a window of opportunity for harvesting root crops, and you want to grab it. Otherwise you will have waited all that time for something that's headed straight to the compost bin.

One season I had a huge harvest of French breakfast radishes waiting for me, but I kept putting off the harvest because I wanted time to pickle them right after picking. When I finally pulled

Root crops take more time than leafy greens to be ready to harvest. But fun fact: all root crops also grow leaves, and these leaves are harvestable and edible almost as soon as they start growing.

DAYS TO HARVEST FOR ROOTS

ROOT CROP	DAYS UNTIL HARVEST
Radishes	35–45
Small carrots and beets	60–80
Celeriac and parsnip	90–100

up the radishes, the roots had grown too large, lost most of their color, and turned fibrous and bitter. I tried to salvage a few as pickles, but the jar sat at the back of the fridge until I finally admitted defeat and tossed them out.

So do as I say and not as I did. Pick your root crops as soon as they show signs of being big enough to eat.

To determine if a root crop is ready, use your finger to sweep around the base of the greens to feel for the top portion of the root known as the "shoulders."

This is the part that pushes up against the topsoil and breaks through when you give the shoots overhead a good tug. If you don't feel anything, the root needs more time to develop, so simply push the soil back in place and check again in a week or two.

Sometimes, ready-to-harvest roots do the work for you and pop their shoulders aboveground. They're not likely to grow much once they're bursting out of the soil, so that makes the decision to pull an easier one.

THE STEP-BY-STEP TO
Harvesting Roots

1 Water the garden well so the soil is moist.

2 Let the water sit overnight.

3 Early in the morning, use a straight hand tool like a hori hori to dig around the area of the root crops.

4 Brush away dirt from the shoulder of each root crop plant to measure its diameter.

5 Gently tug at the stems/base of the root plant and shake it free from the dirt.

6 Rinse in cold water and store in a cool, dry place like a basement or a refrigerator produce drawer.

PRODUCTION

"I'll never take a carrot for granted again." My words after waiting for *months* to pull a little orange piece of magic from my garden beds.

Before we planted our first carrot seeds in Houston, I had no idea what was required to grow these orange things that came in huge plastic bags from the grocery store. It took seasons and seasons of trying, but I finally pulled my first carrot, bent as it was, and felt a new level of respect for something I'd often passed up on the veggie tray or let spoil in the fridge.

This will happen to you too. Planting seeds and hoping they become food will help you see every farmer for what they really are: magicians.

One for one—that's the equation for root plant harvests. For every seed you plant, you'll get one root harvest in return. This quid pro quo for root plants may seem a bit disappointing if you're accustomed to the continuous harvests of cut-and-come-again herbs and salad greens in Steps 1 through 3. But don't forget that you can enjoy the leaves of your root plants the entire time you're waiting for the root harvest. With carrots, radishes, beets, and parsnips, you can cut a few greens here and there from each plant as it grows a bigger root below. But once it's time to pull up the roots, that's the end of the harvest party.

If you hope to harvest a lot of root crops, you'll need to plant a lot of seeds. That's why I've found it's helpful to reserve an entire bed for root crops and to plant the seeds successively over several weeks. If temperatures remain in the optimal range, you can plant new root seeds every 1 to 2 weeks during the growing period.

If you do the math for radishes, you could harvest one row of crops 45 days after the temp hits 55°F, then another row 15 or so days later, and so on. One way to remind yourself to keep sowing seeds is to plant a new row each time you tend the plants that are already established. Alternatively, you could set a schedule to plant a new row every week for 4 weeks in a row.

Root Focus: Radishes

Radishes are the fastest root crop I know. And it's mostly because of their speed that some gardeners claim radishes are the simplest of all garden plants. But I still contend that greens like arugula (which happen to be in the same family) are easier because you don't have to wonder what's happening underground.

When you're ready to step up and grow roots, radishes are the one to try first. Measure 2 inches between each radish seed when you're sowing so you don't have to thin as much later. Radish seeds are tiny—you barely need to cover them with soil. Buried too deep, they'll struggle to reach the surface and might die on their way to sunlight.

Once radishes have produced their first set of true leaves, thin any seedlings without 2 to 3 inches of growing space around them. I've had some luck replanting my thinned radishes if I'm careful with the tender roots while digging and moving them. If you try replanting, keep the transplanted radishes well watered for the first 3 to 5 days in their new garden location.

The first green leaves produced by a radish plant resemble arugula. They even have a similar peppery flavor. Radish leaves are not only edible, but they can also be harvested as you wait for the roots to form.

About 2 weeks after planting, it's helpful to side-dress with fresh finished compost along the roots of the radish plants. This provides a boost of nutrients and gives the roots a little extra cover as they finish growth.

After 40 to 45 days, check the radishes' readiness for harvest. Simply rub your finger around the base of the plant to see if you can feel the shoulders. If you don't feel anything, the radish needs more time to develop. If you feel a firm and round structure, it's time to harvest. Gently tug at the stem of the plant to pull the root up.

The entire radish is edible and should be enjoyed right away. Homegrown radish greens wilt and lose their crispness quickly, but the roots can be plunged in ice water to preserve their crispness after pulling. There are plenty of ways to use radishes in the kitchen. In addition to slicing them up fresh or roasting them, you can pickle and ferment them too—just don't put off harvesting like I did.

Successive sowing won't necessarily result in more crops to harvest overall, but it does result in a steady supply of roots over a span of time, instead of 400 all at once in your bathroom sink. Take a note from my daughters' carrot harvest: it can be difficult (and messy) to handle a large harvest of root crops that's ready all at once.

Fortunately, most root crops store well. Their thick skin, which allowed them to hold nutrients during their growing period, locks in moisture and nutrients during aboveground storage too. Beets, carrots, and larger radishes can be stored in a root cellar (the name fits!) by packing them in sawdust or sand in a container with a lid that's not fully closed. Or you can store these vegetables in the refrigerator for a few weeks before they start to decline in flavor and consistency.

Taking This Step

Learning to grow roots successfully from seed is no small step. Roots are the savings accounts for plants and for the kitchen gardener. They may not be as shiny as perfectly ripe eggplants or impressive like towering stalks of kale, but they're packed with nutrients, last a long time after harvest, and are usually content to keep growing for weeks and months on end even if you pay them no attention.

Even though they're growing down, roots are a step up from growing leaves in the garden. Seeds of root plants take more time to plant and need more help to ensure they germinate. You must control their spacing to be sure each has enough room to mature to full size under the soil surface. And once they're growing, you'll have to pay attention to

Work with Nature

Grow root crops by seed alongside fruit crops from Steps 6 and 7 that take more months to mature. The fast-growing root crops like radishes and carrots provide soil protection and aeration underground as well as an early harvest while you wait on fruiting plants to flower. Just be sure your root crops are well established before the fruiting plants grow tall.

To avoid carrot rust flies and other root crop pests, grow garlic or onion bulbs nearby or plant chives around the border of your root crop garden. Use nasturtiums and calendula as trap crops to keep pests off your root crop greens as they grow.

the signs aboveground to predict what's happening beneath.

It's this combination of more careful attention but low maintenance that makes growing roots the middle part of the gardener's path. On this step, you practice leaning in and noticing the subtle changes in your garden. You decide when to fuss with a plant and when to let it be. And hopefully, you learn to trust nature—that magic is happening even if you can't see it.

Once you watch a tiny seed turn into a thick, sweet, juicy root that you pull from the ground, you'll be hooked and eager to start the next round of seeds so you can experience that rush all over again. But if you think this is magic, just wait till you dig up a potato . . . That's coming up next.

THE STEP-BY-STEP TO
Growing Roots

SET UP

- Create a container or raised bed filled with loose sandy loam soil (see page 69) amended with natural sources of potassium if needed.

- Water the soil well.

- Prepare the seeds for planting.

PLANT

- Space the seeds in rows at least 2 to 4 inches apart.

- Cover lightly with compost.

- Water in gently.

TEND

- Don't allow the soil to dry out before the seeds have fully germinated.

- Keep the soil moist, with at least 1 inch of rain or supplemental water per week applied to the roots.

- Within 2 weeks of planting, thin any plants that were too closely sowed.

- Add organic potassium or phosphorus as a side-dressing to the plants.

- Keep the area free of weeds.

- Hill plants that surface too soon.

- Successively plant new rows of root seeds for a continuous harvest.

HARVEST

- Test the top of each root crop to ensure its width is large enough for harvesting.

- Be sure the garden is not too dry.

- Dig around the base of the plant to loosen the root.

- Gently tug on the root plant's leaves.

- Wash off the roots, dry them, and keep them cool in storage.

Tubers, Bulbs & Rhizomes

"I've been studying plants for dozens of years, and I still learn something new every day." It was summer in Mississippi, and I was walking through the fields with my grandfather, the head of horticulture at Mississippi State. He often brought my sister and me through the campus to see the plants and animals.

I have to admit, back then I was more interested in the pigs and goats than I was the plants. To me, the animals had more personality, and they were just so furry and cute.

Papa was trying to tell me that plants have personality too. It just took me about 30 years to hear him.

When I first started gardening, I figured plant parts were simple: Everything underground was the root. Everything above was the rest of the plant. And while that is mostly true, a lot of other things grow below the surface.

On Step 5 of your gardening journey, you'll learn to grow bulbs, tubers, and rhizomes, each of which has a personality of its own. Each breaks the rules in some form of what we commonly understand about plants.

Start growing any of these, and you might have the same amazement with plants my Papa did.

Just in case you forgot:

Bulb: an underground stem that consists of a bud enclosed in overlapping leaves

Tuber: a fleshy underground stem that can grow new plants through its buds

Rhizome: a horizontal underground stem that can grow lateral shoots

Bulbs, tubers, and rhizomes can all be grown from seed, but they'll mature more quickly and easily when grown from a piece or cutting of the original plant.

Plant Families

There are many plant families you can grow for their bulbs, tubers, and rhizomes, but for the sake of fitting everything into one book, we'll focus on these four.

Amaryllidaceae. Including garlic, onion, and leeks, these are all technically bulbs.

Convolvulaceae, or the morning glory family, includes sweet potatoes and

tons of other species, although not many we eat. Most of them are impractical to grow in a kitchen garden, if not inedible.

Solanaceae. This is the family with potatoes, which, along with sweet potatoes, covers tubers.

Zingiberaceae. This family includes ginger and turmeric, both rhizomes.

Setup

SPACE

Bulbs, tubers, and rhizomes grow large underground while also producing a significant amount of leafy growth aboveground. Throughout their respective growing periods (shortest for potatoes

The Step-by-Step to Planting Potatoes

1 Gather locally sourced organic seed potatoes.

2 Cut the potatoes so that each piece contains at least one eye.

3 Let the potatoes sit overnight for the cut to scab over.

4 Dig 4 to 6 inches and plant a potato eye-side up.

5 Cover with compost and plant another potato with 1 to 1½ feet of space between each.

and longest for garlic and ginger), these plants increase and/or multiply their food stores underground.

Garlic and shallots take one clove and turn it into an entire bulb.

Ginger multiplies and extends one rhizome to become many more.

Potatoes (tubers) and sweet potatoes (tuberous roots) grow new stems from the original tuber, or part of the tuber, and produce new tubers at the end of each stem.

All this underground growth requires extra measuring when planting bulbs and tubers. For bulbs, you plan for vertical growth—the plants won't spread much horizontally. This means you can plant garlic and shallots 4 to 6 inches apart from one another.

For tubers and tuberous roots, expect the plants to reach and stretch horizontally. Give tubers and tuberous roots at least 1 foot to 1½ feet between

each planting. In a raised bed, I typically space each plant about 1 for every 2 square feet, so I can grow 12 plants in 24 square feet. While that spacing would be tight in rows, it works in a raised bed because the roots have more space to spread down.

Rhizomes like ginger should be planted 1 to 2 feet apart.

Before planting bulbs, tubers, and rhizomes, you need to prep both the soil and garden area as well as the plant part itself.

Your goal is large underground stores, so you want to be sure the soil is loose and full of nutrients, with plenty of space for the bulbs and tubers to work their underground magic. These plants can all be grown in a raised bed, a container garden, or even an in-ground row garden. Since these plants stay in the garden for an extended period, I typically avoid placing them in raised beds,

TUBER, BULB, AND RHIZOME FAMILIES AT A GLANCE

FAMILY	COMMON PLANTS
Amaryllidaceae	Shallots, onions, garlic, leeks
Convolvulaceae	Sweet potatoes
Solanaceae	Potatoes
Zingiberaceae	Ginger, turmeric

with the exception of garlic, onions, or shallots planted among my salad plants. Devoting a raised garden to these crops means I won't have frequent harvests from these beds, and multiple harvests are typically my goal because of the easy tending of raised gardens. For that reason, I recommend using additional containers for small quantities of these plants or planting large quantities in a row-garden setup.

If planting in the ground, dig down at least 6 to 12 inches to loosen the soil before planting. Add rich compost in a 1:1 ratio, incorporating it into the existing soil. Be certain the area is free of weeds and nowhere close to a tree or other plant whose roots will compete with your new plants' growth.

To prep bulbs like garlic for planting, start with fully cured organic garlic from the previous year. Use a garden knife to separate each clove from the others, leaving the papery skin intact. Some gardeners choose to soak garlic cloves in a solution of diluted fertilizer for about 12 hours before planting, but I've had plenty of success just planting them as they are.

To prep potatoes for planting, cut a tuber into small sections, making sure there's an eye in each section of the potato. Set these sections out to dry overnight before planting; the scab prevents the tuber from rotting in the soil.

Work with Nature

Plant bulbs like garlic and onions alongside greens, herbs, and root crops to help deter pests. Use flowering herbs like chamomile or calendula to benefit the growth of allium bulbs.

Each season, save your best bulb of garlic, best rhizome of ginger or turmeric, and best potatoes to plant the following season. Your first purchases of these bulbs, tubers, and rhizomes could very well be your last if you grow enough, save a little, and plant again next season.

The best way to prep sweet potatoes is to place a mature sweet potato in moist compost in a cool, dark place. Within a few days, you should see shoots of little green growth, called slips, from the tuber. Let the slips grow for a few more days before cutting each of these tiny plants from the potato, to be planted on its own in the garden area.

Prepping rhizomes isn't quite as complicated. Rhizomes are similar to garlic in taking 9 to 10 months to create an entirely new rhizome like itself. But unlike garlic, most edible rhizomes (like ginger and turmeric) can't survive freezing temperatures. So unless you're in a temperate climate, grow these indoors until the warm season begins and it's safe to plant them outside. Sprout rhizomes for about 6 weeks in seed-starting soil mix indoors. Once you've prepped the soil and plants and confirmed that temperatures are right for what you're planting, it's time to dig holes 4 to 6 inches deep with the proper spacing for each bulb, tuber, or rhizome.

Be sure to place the plant part in the right direction so the leafy growth will be heading up to the soil's surface and not downward. Cover the plant part with loose, compost-rich soil and water in.

SUNLIGHT

When we moved into our new-to-us home in Chicago, I "inherited" a garden box with it. You'd think I'd be happy to find an instant spot for planting, but I recognized instantly that so much of it was wrong.

It was in the wrong location (behind a tree on the south side). It was the wrong size (the bed was over 5 feet wide, which made tending near the middle difficult). And it was too close to the wrong sorts of plants. The previous owner had planted a trumpet vine nearby that continued to send lateral roots into the garden bed.

After trying (unsuccessfully) to plant leaves and fruit plants in this garden, I decided to give it over to garlic instead.

This was wrong too. The worst part? It took me 9 months to find out. (LRF advice: if you're testing out a new garden area, plant plants from Steps 2 and 3 that will tell you if the site is going to work within a few weeks or months.)

The garlic I planted did, in fact, sprout, and I had a good harvest of garlic scapes. Then weeks and months passed. Stalks grew. But they weren't huge and they weren't incredibly green either. I tried to amend the soil and cheer the plants along, but no amount of fertilizer or positive plant affirmations could change the fact that my neighbor's tree was blocking 5 hours of bright summer sunlight from these plants.

At the end of August, 10 months after I'd planted my garlic, I finally gave up and dug in. While each clove had formed a bulb, most were far from impressive in size. The miracle had happened, but just barely.

Lesson learned: only plant bulbs where they'll get good midday sun; otherwise, resign yourself to small bulbs and a long wait that leads to disappointment.

If you can find a spot that receives enough sunlight, your bulbs, tubers, and rhizomes will get the light they need to grow large and nutritious underground. Bulbs like garlic and shallots prefer at least 8 hours, and rhizomes like ginger and turmeric thrive with even more hours of sunlight per day. Tubers and tuberous roots should, if possible, receive 8+ hours of sunlight daily as well. Sweet potatoes can handle every minute of sun you give them, even when it's warm.

So take a note from my inherited garden, and pick a sunny spot, far from other vines, before you dig in.

SEASON

No matter where you're gardening, it's true that there's a bulb, rhizome, or tuber that can always be in the garden. Whether it's garlic setting roots in the middle of winter or sweet potatoes thriving through a red-hot summer, something can always be afoot in a root-based garden.

If you'd like to create a temperature planting calendar, it would read like this:

Potatoes in the Solanaceae family can be planted early in the growing season, as soon as the weather begins to warm and the soil can be worked.

Onions should be started by seed indoors and planted out as soon as the

soil can be worked too (typically when the temps go above 45°F).

Rhizomes for plants like ginger and turmeric can't tolerate frost or snow, so they need to be started indoors and planted after all danger of frost has passed.

Sweet potatoes can only be planted once there's zero chance of frost, and the plants love the long, boiling days of a hot summer. But if you can't give them 100°F heat, at least make sure you have a string of more than 100 days above 80°F on the way.

Some bulbs can be the final thing to plant before winter. Garlic, for instance, does well when planted near the fall equinox. Garlic bulbs won't actually grow and multiply through winter, but the cloves will establish their roots just before the ground hardens with frost; then they'll spend their winter hibernating and settling into their new spot. Once the temperatures warm and the soil reaches above freezing, these bulbs will begin to produce greens.

Given enough sunlight, there's a bulb, tuber, or rhizome from Step 5 that you can grow no matter what time of year. Whether it's garlic hibernating through winter or sweet potatoes multiplying in the heat of summer, magic can be happening right below your feet and not need much from you in the process.

Care

WATER

Bulbs, tubers, and rhizomes are like Goldilocks: they want things to be *just* right. And this includes water.

These plants will need water, but not too little and certainly not too much. Too little and bulbs won't have the energy to swell and store food. Too much and the tubers will rot or mold in the swampy conditions created. The goal is to give these roots a deep watering and then allow the area to dry out before you water again.

When bulbs and tubers near the end of their growing season, stop watering altogether. This allows the bulbs to dry, tighten, and seal themselves for harvest. Harvesting a wet bulb might mean mold or mildew and a short shelf life for your harvest.

Sweet potatoes are the least demanding of water—one of the reasons we recommend them for gardeners who live in extreme heat or who will be traveling. Even so, these drought-tolerant plants will give you more production if they get at least 1 inch of water a week.

Most of these plants will benefit from a formal system of drip irrigation or soaker hoses that ensures the plants get a regular and consistent dose of water. Simply turn the system off when the plants are nearing harvesttime.

Create your bulb garden like the home of the three bears, with settings that are *just right*, and your underground crops will be like Goldilocks: settling in, resting, and growing (until the bears come home).

NUTRIENTS

Similar to roots, the focus for feeding your bulbs, tubers, and rhizomes is on food storage and underground growth. While leaves are important to the plant,

a focus solely on leafy growth can equate to less-than-great growth where it counts.

Just like with root crops, it's preferable to add the necessary nutrients to the planting hole before placing the bulbs and tubers. As the bulb, tuber, or rhizome forms tiny root hairs, those roots will reach farther into the soil beneath them to find the nutrients necessary to support and sustain growth. Placing extra rock phosphate or potash in each planting hole is like packing your kid's lunch for a long day away—you're putting everything they'll need right in the space where they'll reach for it next.

The next time to fertilize the bulbs and tubers with potassium and phosphate would be at the first sign of sprouting. This is often not necessary, but it can speed up bulb or rhizome formation and ensure the plant has all it needs to do the job.

Once the plants begin growing lots of leaves, *do not* add nitrogen-rich fertilizer to the garden area. Let these plants make their own food from the sun and water and surrounding soil. Simply wait to dig up the magic in the months ahead.

TENDING

Most of the tending for bulbs, tubers, and rhizomes is done at the beginning: selecting the best plant parts to start, prepping your growing area, and planting each one properly and at the right temperature. If you take those steps, you're

90 percent of the way there. Then these plants can mostly fend for themselves.

Once bulbs and tubers are planted, be sure they're settled in properly and not rising above the soil surface, and that the soil is not too wet or dry.

You can hill these plants for extra support once the first stems and leaves appear aboveground. Hilling, or adding extra soil or compost around the base of the plant to strengthen root growth, is most important for tubers. In fact, some gardeners swear by the practice of covering the leaves of their potatoes every few weeks because new tubers will grow along the stems of the buried plant parts.

The tending tasks are small, but the rewards for growing underground bulbs and tubers can be huge.

Harvest

TIME

Unlike simple root crops, tubers, bulbs, and rhizomes require more time to size up. A change in leaf color is a telltale sign that the plant is nearing harvesttime. Browning leaves on garlic, potatoes, ginger, and turmeric plants mean your underground treasures are ready to be dug.

One garlic clove will produce stems aboveground that slowly photosynthesize, return energy underground, and eventually produce more cloves around the original clove to form a complete bulb of lots of cloves. Magical, sure, but

the change doesn't happen overnight: it requires up to 9 months in the soil.

For onion bulbs, the growth happens as the onion seed forms a radicle and a green shoot to attract sunlight and water. It takes months for the bulb and stem underground to swell and grow and add more and more layers to the onion. But the waiting is worth it: one tiny seed produces one large, flavorful onion. Another option for growing onions is to plant onion sets. This speeds up the growing time and allows you to start with a small bulb instead of a seed.

For tubers like potatoes and sweet potatoes, one tuber produces both underground and aboveground stems. More tubers form at the edge of each of these stems. Potatoes and sweet potatoes generally require 90 to 120 days to fully mature and be ready for harvest.

By the time you gently dig around the potato or sweet potato plant, you'll find that the tuber piece you planted will now be connected by underground stems to more tubers. It's like a spoke and a wheel that you can eat!

Rhizomes like ginger and turmeric will form stems aboveground; these plants require 8 to 10 months before they're ready for harvest.

Whether it's 90 days or 9 months, the wait for the big dig is well worth it. These plants take a long time because they're doing hard work—creating big stores of food and nutrients that don't just feed the plant but will eventually

The Step-by-Step to Planting Garlic

1 Begin with locally grown organic garlic and prep the bed with compost.

2 Separate each clove, using the largest outer cloves with the skins remaining.

3 Dig a hole 2 to 4 inches deep, and plant the garlic tip-side up.

4 Plant 1 clove every 3 to 4 inches, planting no more than 9 per square foot, and cover with compost.

feed you too. And while this plant is working so hard, you hardly have to do a thing.

Once it's finally time to dig in, be sure to grab your camera. You'll want to watch this one on repeat.

PRODUCTION

It was the last day of school, and the halls were buzzing. You could almost feel the energy of the kids ready to run out the doors that afternoon. And I had the daunting responsibility of hosting my kindergartner's last-day-of-school party. Yikes.

I did the sanest thing I could think of and brought them out into the school garden. Everyone got a brown bag and a small shovel. They were quiet long enough to hear me say, "Start digging!"

Some were confused, and some didn't want to get dirty, but the brave ones got to work. It was quiet at first. I only heard a few of them complaining, "Is this supposed to be a party?"

Then the first cry was heard.

"I found one!" The boy raised his fist in the air with pride. He was holding . . . a potato.

And just like the gold rush, suddenly, the race was on. Everyone now understood the game and began feverishly digging. The shrieks and laughs came quicker and in succession.

"I got one too!"

"This one's huge!"

"Look at this little baby one!"

"Whoa! This one's attached to three more."

The kids filled their bags like it was Halloween, and before we knew it, the bell rang and summer had begun (and I breathed a sigh of relief). I'd survived the kindergartners. But more than that, I'd been reminded of the simple joy we can all find by stepping outside, grabbing a shovel, and getting a little dirty.

When you dig in and pull up your first potatoes or ginger or garlic, you're going to feel like a kid too, and here's what you can expect to find.

Tubers will multiply underground. You can harvest at least 5 or 6 new potato or sweet potato tubers for each tuber you plant. If all has worked as planned, you'll find 5 or more new potatoes attached to the small one you planted months ago.

One hill of a sweet potato plant can yield about 2 pounds of sweet potatoes when the conditions have been just right. A couple of days before harvesting sweet

Bulb Focus: Garlic

Garlic is one-of-a-kind as a root crop. It's planted around the autumn equinox and either lies dormant in winter if you're in a cold climate or creates shoots in winter if you're in a more temperate zone. Garlic requires about 9 months' growing time to harvest.

Garlic comes in two types: hardneck and softneck. Softneck garlic is generally grown in places closer to the equator where the day length stays fairly constant. Hardneck garlic is planted on opposite extremes of the equator, as you get farther north and south.

Plant garlic by breaking a bulb into cloves and setting each clove into the ground separately. Each garlic clove needs at least ⅑ square foot to have enough space to grow into a full bulb. Place the garlic tip pointed up but buried well underground. Garlic can be mulched during winter with extra compost or a bit of straw for protection. Fertilize with potassium-rich fertilizer around the time of planting and again halfway through its growing season.

During the lengthening days of spring, hardneck garlic will produce garlic scapes, which are the first growth of the garlic. Eating the scapes is a delicious way to snag the taste of garlic while you're waiting for the bulb to form.

Each leaf on the garlic stalk represents the growth of one clove. When you see the outer four or five leaves start to brown, this is a sign the garlic is ready for harvest. To harvest, dig around the root of the plant and pull it up all at once. Hang it to dry and cure without getting it wet for at least a few weeks.

After curing, garlic can be stored in a cool, dry place and used all year long until you're ready to harvest the next year's batch.

potatoes, cut the vines above the soil to send the plant's energy toward toughening up the roots, hardening the skin, and sweetening the tubers. After harvesting sweet potatoes, you'll need to cure them. Set them in a warm place in your home and let them rest for a few days before cooking. Curing the tuber settles its sugar content and brightens the flesh. You could also leave some sweet potatoes in the ground and harvest them as you go. Out of the ground, they'll store for 6 to 10 months.

Rhizomes will multiply even more than tubers underground. In fact, some gardeners swear you can pick 20 times more ginger than you plant if it's growing in the right conditions.

Garlic and shallots, though not as impressive as a huge ginger harvest, will still wow you when you tug on a stem and pull up a perfectly shaped bulb, with its sides bulging at each clove and every clove wrapped tightly in a little sliver of skin. To see one little clove disappear into the soil for nearly a year and come up as a complete bulb is nothing short of a miracle.

Taking This Step

I couldn't believe I could feel this angry from a commercial. We were watching TV as a family when an image of kids looking through telescopes at the stars came on our screen.

Overheard was the famous quote from Stephen Hawking: "Look up at the stars and not down at your feet. Be curious."

I heard those words and suddenly felt frustrated.

It's not because I don't love the stars or doubt that there is real magic up there in the Milky Way. But I don't love the fact that our leaders are pointing us to outer space to look for solutions when we're standing on so many of the answers.

Sure, stars are beyond our comprehension and a true marvel. But you can't exactly eat them for dinner.

But a plant that can bury itself underground, multiply tenfold, and then offer itself to me for a meal or two or a dozen is worth looking down at my feet for. Earthy and taken for granted, but no less worthy of awe.

I know it sounds more exciting to shoot for the stars, but maybe we should shoot for the potato instead. When you see what happens as these plants multiply themselves and grow into so much from so little, the feeling is truly out of this world.

In the years to come, I think we'll find that the real frontier has been under our feet the whole time. And the best part? None of us has to board a spaceship to discover it. Don't worry—I'm not mad at my television, but I am more resolved to tell you to be curious *and* look down at your feet.

Shoot for the stars if you want to, but be sure to plant some potatoes before you take off.

Growing Bulbs, Tubers, and Rhizomes

SET UP

- Dig at least 6 to 12 inches in a row garden or raised bed.

- Amend the soil with a 1:1 ratio of freshly finished compost to topsoil.

- Fill the bottom of the planting holes with potash or phosphorus-rich fertilizer.

PLANT

- Place the tubers, rhizomes, or cloves 4 to 6 inches deep and spaced 6 to 12 inches apart, with roots pointed down.

- Cover with 4 inches of compost-amended soil.

- Water in well.

TEND

- Water 1 inch per week, only if necessary.

- Hill the compost or soil around the main stems of the plants, but not too high.

- Keep the area weed free.

HARVEST

- Begin harvesting when the leaves start to turn brown or fall over.

- Leave the bulbs, tubers, and rhizomes in a cool, dry place to cure before consuming.

part four **fruit**

"How long till we get there?"
We were driving home, away from my
mom's garden, where my children had
plucked those cherry tomatoes from the
vine and made me say those four words,
"I want a garden." It had already been
a long road trip, and it wasn't just my
kids asking if we were there yet. I was
itching to get home, till up the backyard,
plant some tomatoes, and eat food I'd
grown myself.

It was more than a six-hour drive, but the journey to my first tomato harvest took way longer. In fact, six summers passed before I had my first official tomato victory.

One spring, after I'd figured out oregano, lettuce, carrots, and potatoes, I knew I was finally ready to have my own basketful of homegrown tomatoes. My beds were set up, I'd learned which trellis system I could use to get the most tomatoes possible in my raised beds, and I had a list of the best varieties I'd grow.

I knew I could grow at least 30 tomato plants in 2 beds using the Florida weave trellising system, sandwiching the plants between supportive rows of twine. I planted the tomatoes early, as soon as the last frost date had passed. I set up drip hoses along each row of tomatoes, and made a fertilizing and pruning plan. I'd learned the year before to prune the leaves more thoroughly, and I gathered some earthworm castings and chicken manure, which I vowed to use each weekend once the plants started flowering.

I stuck with it. Every Saturday before the kids got up, I'd head outdoors with my pruners, gloves, and worm poo. I'd cut back the lowest leaves, sprinkle a few castings around each plant, and water well. The rest of the week, I'd take a break and watch the plants grow by the day. As soon as another Saturday rolled around, I was back at it.

Within 60 days, I had my first tomato harvests, and the fruit kept coming every week thereafter. I was making salsa and sauces and eating caprese like it was my

full-time job. I had so many tomatoes by my kitchen sink that I was calling neighbors to come and take some.

It was too late to be beginner's luck. I hadn't gotten a degree, read a certain book, or suddenly acquired lots of land. This was simply the result of five years of growing lots of simpler plants, learning how plants work step by step, and enjoying smaller harvests of leaves and roots. Oh, and also not giving up.

If you've made it this far, perhaps you feel like you've been on a very long road trip too, wondering when you'd finally make it to the tomatoes.

Good news! You're here!

And since you're reading this book, I'm hoping it won't take you six years to reach this point. But even if it does, know that you're not alone. In this step, you'll learn all that I learned to reach my first year of tomato success (and what I've figured out since then too).

So no more asking, "How long till we get there?"—okay?

Let's jump out and start planting.

STEP 6

Small Fruit

You may be thinking of apples and oranges when you hear the word *fruit*, but because you're reading this book, you now know that most of the plants you're hoping to grow in your "vegetable garden" aren't actually "vegetables" after all—they're fruits.

Fruit is the often sweet, fleshy product of a plant that contains seeds and can be eaten as food.

And good news: this means when you ask your kids if they'd prefer fruit or vegetables for dinner and they say, "Fruit" (like mine always do), you can pile their plates with squash, zucchini, tomatoes, and beans. They asked for it.

If we refer to the life stages of a plant (see page 10), we know that fruit develops near the end of the life cycle, right before the plant starts all over again with seeds.

It wasn't until I mapped out each step of this system that I realized there needed to be a distinction between small and large fruit. The reason? Because a fruit that weighs ¼ pound has different needs as far as sun, space, time, and tending from one that weighs 4 or even 40 pounds.

Also, many of us have enough room, even with just 16 or so square feet of growing space, to grow a lot of small fruit, but we could use up nearly all our space with just one or two large-fruiting plants if we don't know better.

I know for myself, with a raised-bed garden that has under 100 square feet of growing space, that growing large fruit has not been a priority. But with intensive planting methods, I'm able to pack lots of small-fruiting plants in my raised beds and enjoy harvests all season long.

So let's begin with small fruit, but don't forget about my epic tomato harvest. Just because we call them small doesn't mean their production is insignificant.

Side note: Where to draw the line between small and large fruit is a tough one. For this book and in the hope of simplicity, the tipping point was a plant that needed more than 3 square feet of growing space in a raised-bed garden and/or required or could produce fruit after 120 days of growing. I also used the weight of the fruit as an indication of whether it's in the small or large category. As with almost anything in the garden, it's debatable!

Plant Families

We consider some of the fruiting plants from the following three families small

EGGPLANT

BUSH BEAN

YELLOW BELL PEPPER

CUCAMELON

TOMATO

SHISHITO PEPPER

'SUNGOLD' TOMATO

'BLUE LAKE' BUSH BEAN

CROOKNECK SQUASH

BANANA PEPPER

TOMATILLO

'FAIRY TALE' EGGPLANT

because (a) their fruit won't weigh more than a few pounds, (b) most finish growing within 60 to 100 days of planting, and (c) they require less than 2 to 3 square feet to grow to maturity.

Solanaceae. This family, also called the nightshade or tomato family, is perhaps the best known of the fruiting plant families. You met potatoes in Step 5; now it's time to meet tomatoes, peppers, ground-cherries, tomatillos, and small eggplants.

These plants all grow quite large, and some, like vining tomatoes and tomatillos, grow quite tall. These plants produce fruit from their pretty little flowers and grow mostly in the warm or hot seasons.

Cucurbitaceae. This family includes cucumbers, squash, and zucchini, plus large-fruiting plants that we'll cover in Step 7. Plants in this family take up lots of space and either grow in a bush-like or a vining form.

Fabaceae. This family is also referred to as the legume family and includes peas and beans, which grow their seeds inside pods that emerge from flowers. Yes, peas and beans are considered fruit—unless you let them grow till they turn brown and dry, when they're considered seeds (more on that in Step 8).

Malvaceae. This family includes okra and roselle, as well as cotton and hibiscus. These heat-loving plants grow tall and produce beautiful flowers that then produce fruit full of seeds.

Setup

SPACE

Once upon a time, my four children shared one room. We set up two bunk beds, and every night felt like a slumber party. It was a little magical and a lot chaotic. It was also efficient. I put them all to bed at the same time, got all my goodnight kisses within 6 feet of space, and woke them up together.

Fast-forward a year or two, and things weren't so simple. The little feet that

SMALL-FRUIT FAMILIES AT A GLANCE

FAMILY	COMMON BUSH PLANTS	COMMON VINE PLANTS
Cucurbitaceae	Squash, zucchini	Cucumbers
Fabaceae	Bush beans, peas	Pole peas and beans
Malvaceae	Okra, roselle	—
Solanaceae	Peppers, determinate tomatoes, ground-cherries, eggplants	Indeterminate tomatoes, tomatillos

once crawled into the bunks were bigger, as were the attitudes. They all wanted space to spread out.

Don't they say that kids grow like weeds? What works when kids are young is so different from what works when they're older. The same is true for plants. When plants are just producing leaves, they're like toddlers in bunk beds—it may be a little chaotic, but you can squeeze them in tight. But as they age and continue growing, they will want a place to stretch out and you'll prevent a lot of fights if you give them what they're asking for.

We learned this lesson the hard way when we first tried to grow cucumbers. Jason carefully situated a big pot on the upper deck of our rental and planted the seeds just as the package instructed (he's better at following directions than I am).

The seeds sprouted within a few days, and the vines started to grow, three or four in all. The plan was perfect: cucumbers right outside the kitchen door.

The cucumbers didn't agree. Within weeks, the vines had coiled around each other, and before we knew it, the pot looked like the kids' playroom: a complete and total mess.

Lesson learned: for that size pot, only a single cucumber seed was needed. This is a truth we just don't want to believe when we open a seed packet and spot dozens of beautiful seeds inside. How can you plant *just one*?

Fruiting plants have a sweet and heavy burden to bear: growing and ripening a casing full of pulp, seeds, and juice, which weighs so much more than leaves. The plant stems need to be thicker, the roots need more space to spread and burrow deep, and the plant itself needs plenty of room to grow aboveground—all to support the weight of this growth.

In short, give these plants plenty of space if you want them to give you plenty of fruit.

Fruiting plants take up space aboveground in one of two ways: by growing long or wide.

Many fruiting plants grow long on indeterminate vines. The word *indeterminate* means what it sounds like: not yet determined. In other words, these vines can be 6, 7, even 10 feet long. Remember what makes a plant a plant? It can grow forever.

Small fruiting plants with indeterminate vines include tomatoes and tomatillos in the Solanaceae family, cucumbers and certain types of squash (like winter squash) in the cucurbit family, and pole beans in the Fabaceae family.

These plants need to grow up or grow out. You can either give them a structure to climb up and grow tall on, or you have to be willing to give over almost your entire bed so the vines can spread on the ground. My recommendation? Use a raised bed and trellis on which the plant can cling to double your productive space. With that type of setup, you can allot each plant as little as 12 to 18 inches in width.

Other fruiting plants grow wide instead of long. These plants include zucchini and squash, peppers, determinate tomatoes, eggplants, broccoli and cauliflower, and large eggplants (some of which you'll learn in Step 7). Even though they don't need something to climb on, they may need stakes or small trellises to support their bulk and keep them upright.

Zucchini and squash tend to take up the most horizontal space in the garden. These plants need a minimum of 1 full square foot, though they prefer more like 2 to 3 square feet per plant.

For this reason, I often plant these outside my raised beds, in more of a row-garden style.

SUNLIGHT

If you've ever had a tomato, cucumber, or pea vine that grew loads of leaves but hardly any fruit, lack of sunlight might be the reason.

Fruiting plants require warm soil and long days of sunshine to reach their full potential, so grow them in places that receive 8 or more hours of direct sun. These plants need energy to not only produce stems, leaves, and flowers but also form and ripen fruit.

Ensure your plants receive enough sun by first setting your plants to face south (north if in the Southern Hemisphere). If setting plants on a trellis, consider positioning it in an east–west direction so one side of the trellis isn't shading another.

When interplanting fruiting plants with others, provide plenty of space between each seed so the resulting plant receives sunlight on as many of its leaves as possible. As the plants grow each week, prune back extra branches so that each plant gets its own share of sunlight.

SEASON

A solstice to an equinox, or an equinox to a solstice—that's how much time is needed for most small-fruiting plants to finish their production. I know I'm speaking Latin here, so let me explain.

An equinox occurs in spring and fall when the daytime is equal to the night (both 12 hours). A solstice is when the sun is at the highest point (summer) or lowest point (winter) in the sky, resulting in the longest or shortest day of the year. The time between a solstice and an equinox is about 90 days, or 3 months, and your small-fruiting plants need about that long to finish their production. Peas, for example, are often planted at spring equinox and harvested at summer solstice.

Before I began gardening, I paid no attention to full moons or the first day of spring. Every day at the office seemed the same. But when I started gardening, the solstice and the equinox suddenly mattered a great deal.

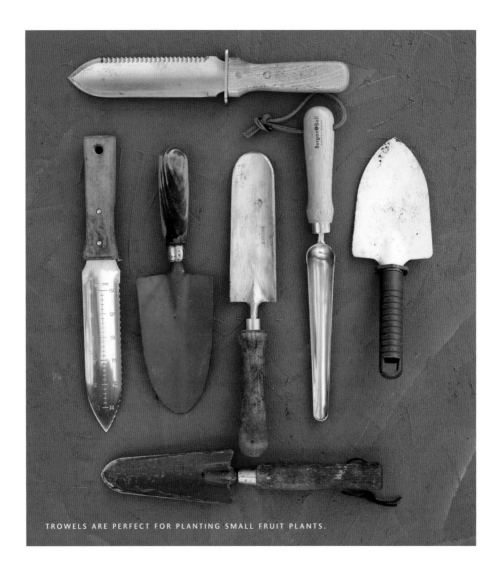

TROWELS ARE PERFECT FOR PLANTING SMALL FRUIT PLANTS.

The solstice is typically the time to plant seeds. Winter solstice is the time to start cool-season fruiting seeds indoors for spring planting in cool climates and warm-season fruiting seeds for warmer climates. Spring equinox is the time to plant all those seedlings outdoors and start fruiting plants for summer (warm season and hot season) indoors. By summer solstice, all the previous fruiting plants should be removed (cool-season plants in cooler climates and warm-season plants in warmer climates). The next season's fruiting plants (warm-season plants in cooler climates and hot-season plants in warmer climates) should

Work with Nature

Plant flowering herbs from the Asteraceae family near small-fruiting plants to attract bees and butterflies to the flowers of tomato, cucumber, or squash plants, which need pollination. Allow herbs like cilantro, dill, parsley, and basil to flower in the garden and attract even more pollinating creatures. African blue basil is one of the most attractive herbs for pollinating insects.

Plant trap crops like nasturtium and calendula to deter pests from your fruiting crops.

Add still water features like birdbaths for creatures to drink so they're less likely to puncture your fruit for water.

Grow leafy greens and shallow-rooted herbs around fruiting plants to protect the soil, to provide additional harvests as you wait for the fruit to finish production, and to aerate the surrounding soil.

Plant natives and grasses near your garden space to provide habitat for beneficial insects and local birds and wildlife that will feast on pests that prey on fruiting plants.

be planted out in the garden and getting ready to produce their first flowers.

Between each period of solstice to equinox or equinox to solstice, small-fruiting plants will start producing fruit 55 or 60 days from planting and keep producing for another 30 to 45 days if conditions stay optimal. This means you'll be harvesting small cool-season fruit up until spring equinox in warm climates and then cool-season fruit in cooler climates and warm-season fruit in warmer climates up until summer solstice.

Around the fall equinox, warm-season plants are removed in cooler climates and hot-season plants removed in warmer climates, and then fall-fruiting

plants are installed. By the winter solstice, the cool-season fruiting plants are pulled from cooler climates and planted in warmer climates, and the cycle begins all over again.

A few fruiting plants, like broccoli, cauliflower, sugar snap peas, and snow peas, grow in the cool season. All other fruit performs best in warm and hot seasons, when temperatures stay regularly above 75°F but before they exceed 90°F.

Warm-season fruits, like tomatoes, peppers, cucumbers, and squashes, have zero frost tolerance. These plants need to be planted after the threat of frost has passed in your area, or under cover that protects your plants from frost or snow.

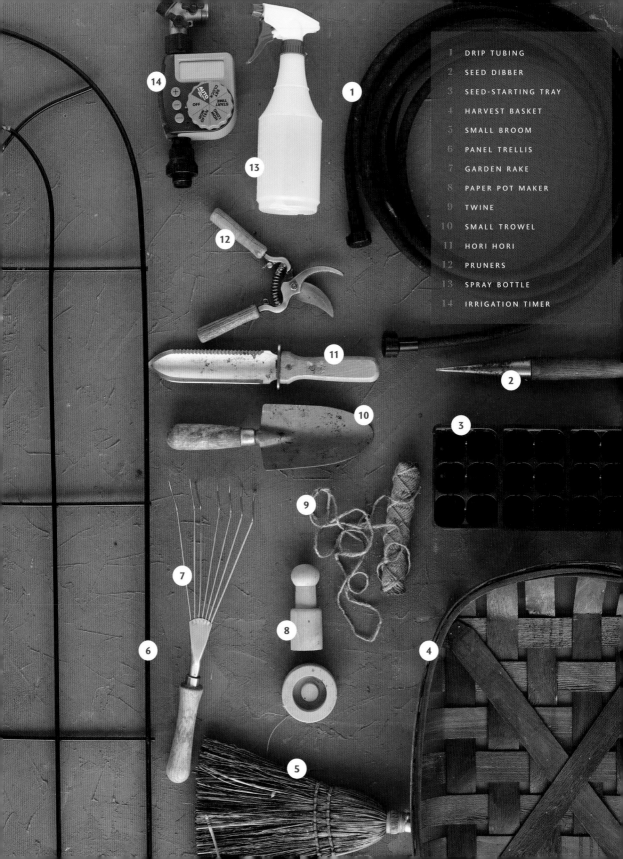

1 DRIP TUBING

2 SEED DIBBER

3 SEED-STARTING TRAY

4 HARVEST BASKET

5 SMALL BROOM

6 PANEL TRELLIS

7 GARDEN RAKE

8 PAPER POT MAKER

9 TWINE

10 SMALL TROWEL

11 HORI HORI

12 PRUNERS

13 SPRAY BOTTLE

14 IRRIGATION TIMER

Care

WATER

I can still remember sending a picture of a pile of cucumbers—there must have been 20 in the frame—to Jason.

"Too bad we can't eat any of these," I wrote, adding a frowny-face emoji for good measure.

We'd finally figured out how much space our cucumbers needed, and we'd given it to them. We planted a row of seeds along the edge of the garden bed where they'd receive plenty of sun, and rigged a panel trellis of rebar and netting to support the vines as they grew up and up and up some more. It seemed our efforts were paying off when a canopy of leaves appeared, and then, even better, loads of baby cucumbers formed behind flowers.

There was only one problem.

The cucumbers weren't edible. Well, technically, you could eat them. One bite wouldn't kill you, but it would certainly make your nose scrunch and your eyes water as you fought the temptation to spit it out. These cucumbers were extremely bitter and destined for one spot: the compost pile.

I knew I hadn't watered the cucumbers the way I was supposed to when they were planted, but I had no idea that missing a few days of watering would mean all those beautiful plants would be for looks only.

You can do everything else right with fruiting plants, but if you get the water

wrong, you might end up spitting out the fruit you've worked so hard to grow.

While all plants need water at the beginning of their life cycle to germinate, fruiting plants need a lot of water in the middle period when they begin to flower and fruit. In fact, most fruit is over 80 percent water, which means a consistent watering schedule is critical as you near and complete the fruiting stage.

After watering your plants every other day when they're first transplanted to the garden, you'll switch to giving them one deep watering per week (6 to 8 weeks in). At least 1 inch of water aimed at the roots per week should do it. Measuring rainfall will help you determine when the rain has covered your water duty for you.

WINTER SOLSTICE
Start first-season fruiting plants indoors (cool/warm); pull last-season fruiting plants from the garden (cool/warm).

SPRING EQUINOX
Plant out first-season fruiting plants (cool/warm); start next-season fruiting plants indoors (warm/hot).

SUMMER SOLSTICE
Plant out next-season fruiting plants (warm/hot); start third-season fruiting plants indoors (cool/warm); pull first-season fruiting plants (cool/warm).

FALL EQUINOX
Plant out next-season fruiting plants (cool/warm); start next-season fruiting plants indoors if in a temperate climate (cool); pull previous season's fruiting plants (warm/hot).

You'll know if your watering schedule has not been consistent by looking at the fruit. If it bursts open, cracks, peels, or rots, that's usually a sign that the water was off—either too much, too little, or too inconsistent. (We're on Step 6 here; I warned you!)

NUTRIENTS

All-purpose fertilizer is often suggested for growing plants of any type, especially fruiting ones. While I must admit the one-and-done method of feeding your plants sounds super appealing, I wouldn't recommend it.

Think about nature. A plant in the wild rarely sits on loads of nutrients all at once. Instead, the plant may start growing in surface-level nitrogen-rich leaf mold from the winter before. Then, as its roots push farther into the ground, they reach the potassium-rich potash that's left from trees burning years ago. And finally, when the plant begins to flower and fruit, its roots dig deeper and encounter rock phosphate, the remnant of rocks that settled a long, long time ago. Isn't nature the best thing?

This simple picture of a plant in the wild reminds us that plants have different nutritional needs at distinct stages of their life cycle. Feeding your plant with all-purpose fertilizer is like setting a plate of steak, potatoes, and salad on your baby's high chair tray right next to her bottle of milk. Sure, she might eventually need or want everything on that plate, but for now, the milk is all she can handle.

If you're simply growing leaves, you can provide the same nutrients throughout the plant's entire productive life cycle. But each additional stage of plant growth comes with a need for more and different nutrients. That means you'll feed fruiting plants in stages. Every time the plant does something new, give it something new to eat.

Apart from beans and peas, most fruiting plants need mostly nitrogen at the beginning of their growth cycle to start growing stems and leaves. As they become stronger and taller, all fruiting plants can benefit from more potassium and calcium for a healthy root system.

Then, if you've gotten everything right, the first flower appears. This is your sign to stop feeding the plant nitrogen and begin to feed the plant something new, and that something is phosphorus. Photosynthesis will be in full swing at this point, and your plant will instinctively grow more (and more) leaves. More nitrogen at the flowering stage will keep your plant in leaf-production mode rather than fruiting mode.

How do you add more phosphorus to your plant's environment? For fast absorption, you can spray the leaves with a diluted organic liquid. But my favorite method is to side-dress the plant with an organic granular mixture, which allows for a slower uptake from the roots. This way, I know exactly how much food each

plant is receiving, I know that nutrients will reach the roots first, and I'm less tempted to overtreat the plant.

Of course, you can simply place a layer of finished compost around the fruiting plants. Again, think about nature. Picture a fruiting plant in the wild growing next to other, shorter-lived plants. The fruiting plant will be going strong 60 to 75 days in while the shorter-lived plants complete their life cycle, decompose, and enrich the soil just at the time the fruiting plants need more nutrients to grow taller and fruit.

Any time I see the soil around my plants turning a lighter shade of brown or looking more dry or sandy than usual, I add an inch or two of compost around the base of each fruiting plant. This provides extra space for the roots to spread out, retains moisture, and releases more

Typical Causes of Fruit Issues

- Deformed fruit—potassium deficits, though nitrogen excess can contribute
- Blossom-end rot (tomatoes)—lack of calcium
- Lack of flowers or dropped flowers—lack of phosphorus
- Fruit not fully formed—lack of pollination

nutrients to the plant in the safest way—the way nature does.

TENDING

There's a reason I saved fruiting plants for Steps 6 and 7. The carefree days of cutting a few herbs while you're waiting for potatoes to be ready are over. Most of these fruiting plants need your care, right now, next week, and the week after that too.

These plants need pruning. They need feeding. They need support. They need attention!

Don't worry. A little effort goes a long way, but fair warning: once you start tending, it's hard to stop. These plants ask a lot but can give you plenty in return. Once you're carrying baskets of sweet, juicy tomatoes, piles of fresh beans, or a bucket of cucumbers inside (hopefully yours are edible!), you'll barely remember all you had to do to get there.

Besides watering, Step 6 in your gardening progress requires heavy pruning for some fruiting plants in a way you haven't experienced in previous steps. Sure, you trim back salad greens and herbs, but each of those snips is really a form of harvesting. With fruiting plants, you toss what you prune in the compost bin, knowing, however, that each cut likely means more fruit to eat and enjoy later.

Your tool for the job is a set of clean pruners.

Just as you did for leaves and roots, you'll cut away from the fruiting plants any leaves that are discolored or spotted

Small-Fruit Tending Schedule

WEEKS 1 AND 2

- Water every other day.
- Feed with compost or a nitrogen fertilizer.
- Prune away damaged leaves; prune indeterminate vines to one main stem; allow bush varieties to branch out as they naturally do.
- Protect seedlings with garden mesh.
- Install a trellis at least 6 feet tall for vining varieties and install a plant stake or tomato cage at least 3 feet tall for bush varieties.

WEEKS 3 AND 4

- Water every other day.
- Feed with compost or a potassium fertilizer.
- Prune away damaged leaves.
- Protect small plants with garden mesh or weather cloth.
- Attach vines or branches to a trellis (indeterminate/vine) or plant support (determinate/bush).

WEEKS 5 TO 10

- Water once a week, 1 inch per week.
- For vining varieties, keep the bottom pruned to one main stem; prune below the first flower; prune a third of the lower leaves.
- For bush varieties, allow the plant to branch out as much as possible; prune only damaged or discolored leaves.
- Feed with phosphorus and calcium.
- Attach new vining growth to a trellis for support.
- Protect the growing plants with a physical barrier.
- Pick fruit as soon as it begins to ripen.

WEEKS 11 TO 14

- Water once a week, 1 inch per week.
- Top off indeterminate vines; allow bush varieties to continue to grow.
- Feed with phosphorus and calcium.
- Pick ripening fruit daily.

one main stem. Think of your fruiting plant as a mini tree. You don't see many mature trees that last for decades with a lot of trunks. There's usually a thick main trunk, and the rest of the plant's extensive growth springs from that one source. The same works for your fruiting plants.

Although leaves are critical for plant health, our second pruning goal is to retain the fewest leaves possible on indeterminate fruiting plants. Why? Each leaf contains cells that need support, water, and other nutrients at the expense of more flowers and fruit; each leaf blocks some airflow; and each leaf grabs sun that could be landing on—and ripening—the fruit instead.

The more leaves grow on a fruiting plant, the more the plant will delay or slow its fruiting. That's why regularly pruning, weekly or biweekly, the lower and outer leaves, never more than one-third of the plant at a time, is critical to get the most fruit until the plant slows its growth near day 75 to 90 in the garden. At this stage, the plant is likely full of fruit, much of which will have yet to ripen.

Now it's time to prune to encourage the plant to stop producing new fruit and to start ripening the fruit already on the vine. This process is called "topping," because you prune the top of the plant. Through topping, you tell the plant to direct its energy to finish forming and ripening the fruit (so you can pick it) before the optimal season is over.

or that have holes or tears. These leaves are most likely suffering from pests or disease, and it's usually best to throw them out or compost them in a separate pile that you won't use for your edible garden.

Pruning is also a way to tell your plants what you want from them: more fruit and fewer leaves and stems. If you let the plant grow on its own, the plant may keep producing more stems and leaves instead of flowering or fruiting until the season has nearly come to an end. But pruning directs the plant to slow its leaf growth and move to the fruiting stage sooner rather than later— giving you more fruit throughout the growing period.

Pruning is recommended for indeterminate tomato, cucumber, and pole bean vines. The first pruning goal is to identify

THE STEP-BY-STEP TO

Pruning Indeterminate Tomatoes, Cucumbers, and Beans

1   If the plant branches out at the base, prune to one main stem within 2 to 3 weeks of planting by selecting the largest stem to be the main provider. Prune back any new stems that sprout from the base of the plant.

2   Prune all leaves and stems below the first flower when it appears.

3   Every 2 weeks, prune the lower leaves on the vine, removing about a third of the plant's leaves.

4   Prune suckers (new vines that form between the main stem and lateral branches) if you want larger fruit, and leave suckers if you'd like more fruit.

5   Two to 3 weeks before the season changes, top off plants so existing fruit will finish.

I wish I could say your tending tasks end there. But because you've made it this far, I can talk straight with you: Your fruit is now in danger. Serious danger. There are lions and tigers and bears (oh my!) coming for your fruit.

Well, maybe not lions and tigers, but the bears would definitely come for it if they could cross the road without being spotted.

More so than with roots and greens, just about every animal within eyesight or smelling distance will hunt ripe garden fruit. Microscopic insects, four-legged beasts (aka deer), and everything in between will come from below, from above, and at eye level.

And what do you do about the pests?

1   Use a physical barrier.

2   Think about nature and find the pest's predator.

3   Create an ecosystem.

4   Hire a full-time security guard.

The most successful way to prevent pests from eating fruit is to create a physical barrier.

To protect your garden from mice, gophers, voles, chipmunks, and other tunneling animals, place a layer of hardware cloth at the bottom of your garden beds. This metal cloth can be stapled to the bottom of wooden raised beds before you add soil and plants. To protect fruit above the ground, use a protective cover, installing a cage or mesh cover over the bed that will keep the fruit in and the pests out.

While there are all kinds of recommended sprays and guerrilla tactics for battling pests, my best success, after all these years, has come from simply putting up physical barriers around fruiting plants, like mesh, cages, and fences. The animals that want to eat from your garden are smart, so a physical barrier they can't get through is often the only way to keep them off your fruit.

Next, pay attention to the ecological system surrounding the garden.

Let me explain.

Remember the tomato-stealing raccoon? Because I didn't know to do all the things you've learned so far, we had only about 10 tomatoes growing—nowhere near enough to feed both the raccoon and us! So I promptly went to the local garden center and explained my dilemma.

"Buy some coyote urine," the lady told me with a straight face.

Before I could ask if the store even had coyote urine and, if so, how they had obtained such a thing, she explained that raccoons are scared to death of coyotes.

One whiff of their predator's presence in the garden, and those raccoons would hightail it out of our yard, leaving the precious tomatoes unscathed.

I must admit I passed on buying the coyote urine that day, but I learned a lesson money couldn't buy. When your tomatoes become some animal's prey, it's time to go out and find that animal's predator. Every predator has a predator. You learned that in fourth-grade science—remember the food web?

Food chains begin with autotrophs (i.e., the plants in your garden that produce their own food). Primary consumers, usually herbivores, eat the autotrophs. I wish you had the privilege of being the only primary consumer in your garden, but it's just as likely to be a squirrel. So your job is to work with nature and think about what animals want to eat the animals that want to eat from your garden. Squirrels are eaten by owls, snakes, coyotes, and homesteaders (just kidding about the last one). If you have too many squirrels and not enough owls, snakes, or coyotes, you'll likely end up with not enough garden. So the trick is to introduce the presence of a predator or the *suggestion of the presence of a predator* as soon as possible.

Once you know what wildlife would naturally eat the problem prey, either welcome the predator into your garden, if you dare, or find ways to imitate that predator's behavior in a way that tells the prey a predator is ready to pounce should he even think about stepping inside your garden bed. This can be as simple as welcoming ladybugs into your garden when the prey is another insect and as complex as bringing in owls (for squirrels) or even dogs for bigger predators like raccoons, squirrels, or rabbits.

Need an owl? Install an owl box. (We did this with great success in a large pine tree.) Or simply purchase a plastic owl and place it in the garden area.

Need more ladybugs? Take time to learn what plants ladybugs love and what type of environment they reproduce in, and create a garden space that's suited for them.

Need a person? You could hire your children to stand guard in the garden 24 hours a day, or you could build a scarecrow.

Need a coyote? I suggest you just let your dog (or the neighbor's) run free and regularly lift his leg in the garden instead.

Whatever you do, don't let all that hard work you've done to start a plant from seed and grow it tall end up in the belly of any creature other than yourself. Use physical barriers and create ecosystems that work with nature, support the health of your plants and the overall environment, and result in more harvests for you (and fewer for the squirrels).

Harvest

PRODUCTION

If you've never seen a pepper plant before, it's easy to assume that growing one plant each season will supply so

much fruit that you'll never have to buy peppers from the store again. This is true only if you don't really like peppers and rarely eat them. Because one pepper plant, even at its healthiest, will likely only produce 8 to 10 peppers.

When it comes to production, the truth is that most of us vastly *under*estimate the amount of leaves one plant will grow but *over*estimate the amount of fruit one plant can produce in a single season. Let me break it to you: one pepper plant is not going to grow enough for you in one season.

Fruiting plants don't produce fruit the minute they're planted; they need to get established with deep roots, a strong main stem, and lots of leaves before

Small Fruit Focus: Tomatoes on an Arch Trellis

Growing tomatoes up an arch trellis is kinda my thing. In my opinion, there are few accomplishments in the garden more exciting than when two tomato plants meet at the top of an arch. I love the beauty of the vines forming a mini jungle along the trellis and taking a walk under their fruit clusters.

Here's how to grow tomatoes on an arch trellis.

1   Set up the arch trellis and plant indeterminate tomatoes. (My favorite varieties are 'Sungold', 'Juliet', and 'Black Cherry'.)

2   Prune the plant to one main stem and continue to prune weekly. This tells the plant to put its energy into ripening the tomatoes rather than growing more leaves. It's up to you to decide if you'll prune the suckers to get *bigger* tomatoes or leave the suckers to get more tomatoes. (I do the latter.)

3   Support the tomato plants as they grow by tying the vines with twine along the trellis rungs or slats.

4   Water deeply and add organic phosphorus fertilizer weekly once plants start to flower.

5   Top off the tomato plants as you near the end of the growing season: Cut off the very top of the vine to tell the plant to stop putting energy into growing bigger and to put all its energy into finishing the fruiting process. This encourages green fruit to ripen as quickly as possible. If fruit on the vine needs to be harvested because frost is coming or squirrels are stealing your harvest, cut the clusters and bring them indoors to rest on a windowsill or ripen inside a brown bag. But I prefer the flavor when fruit is kept on the vine as long as possible.

6   Remove the tomato vines from the kitchen garden after they have enjoyed 90 to 100 days growing over the trellis. By now they are past their optimal growth time, and the garden will do better if you replace the tired vines with younger plants. Leaving tomato vines on the trellis too long often welcomes pests and disease into your kitchen garden.

they'll even start to flower. Why all this prep work? Because plants are smart. They want to hedge their bets, so they're not going to fruit until they know the conditions are right for making as many seeds as they possibly can.

Don't rush with fruiting plants. Instead, focus on what the plant cares most about at each stage of its growth: feeling at home, growing strong, and preparing for the best production. Make growing conditions optimal and give fruiting plants the strongest structure possible so that when a plant is finally ready, it will produce as much sweet fruit as it possibly can. You may not be able to stop buying from the grocery store, but you will get to taste the best fruit possible, even if there are only a handful to try.

Once small-fruiting plants have been in the garden for about 60 days, you should expect fruit to form. Most small-fruiting plants need to finish their life cycle before 100 to 120 days (remember: equinox to solstice or solstice to equinox), so a plant only has around 1 month, 2 at most, left to produce enough fruit to do what it came here to do: create many more members of its species.

If your plant is not forming and ripening fruit between days 60 and 90 in the garden, something is off. Review the tending notes and decide if you need to add nutrients, prune more heavily, or adjust the watering.

ESTIMATED HARVESTS PER SMALL-FRUIT PLANT

PLANT	SIZE OF FRUIT	NUMBER OF FRUIT PER PLANT	RECOMMENDED NUMBER OF PLANTS PER PERSON
Cherry tomatoes	1/20 pound	200	2
Large tomatoes	1/2 to 1 pound	30	4
Peppers	1/4 to 1/2 pound	20	3
Cucumbers	1/2 to 1 pound	10	6
Squash	1 pound	5	2
Zucchini	1 pound	5	2
Eggplant	1 pound	8	2
Peas	1/16 pound	30	30

Taking This Step

That spring of my first big tomato success, a funny thing happened to my hands. One Saturday morning, when I'd finished my weekly ritual of pruning dozens of tomato leaves, fertilizing, and watering, I had to take a second to look at my fingers. They were slightly discolored—from my fingertips to the creases of my palms.

What color were they? The most wonderful shade of tomato-leaf green.

As I looked out on my healthy and fruiting tomato plants, I had to laugh to myself. "So *this* is how you get a green thumb?"

That's when it all made sense. Becoming a gardener isn't something that happens in an instant. Gardening isn't sorcery or magic that some of us are naturally endowed with. It's simply a system: first leaves, then roots, then fruit. The more I understood the way plants worked in the garden, the less work I needed to do as a gardener.

After six years, dozens of growing seasons, and countless withered tomato vines, my thumb was actually turning green.

The work of pruning, trellising, and harvesting in Step 6 can be a little time-consuming, and you might find yourself wondering around day 75: *Am I doing this right?* But as long as you don't give up, you'll soon look down and discover your own green thumb too.

Growing Small Fruit

SET UP

- Set up raised garden beds that are 12 to 18 inches tall, and then fill with 103 soil blend (see page 69).

- Install an automated or simple watering system like drip hoses or low-emitter spray heads.

- Install protective cover structures such as hardware cloth, garden hoops, or garden fences.

PLANT

- Dig holes for fruiting plants that are the depth of each transplant and twice its width.

- Install plant supports like trellises to support vining and large plants.

- Add transplants and/or seeds in the garden in designated spots along trellises with ample space between plants.

- Water in thoroughly.

TEND

- Water every other day for the first 2 weeks and maintain at least 1 inch of water per week during growing.

- Fertilize all but beans and peas with organic nitrogen in the first few weeks of growth, and then add potassium and phosphorus at the time of flowering and fruiting.

- Prune plants regularly to prevent disease or decay and promote fruit growth.

- Trellis or support vining and large plants once per week.

- Protect plants from pests and/or weather with physical barriers and protective measures.

HARVEST

- Harvest the first fruit as soon as they show signs of ripeness.

- Pick ripening fruit weekly to encourage more production.

- Top off the plants 2 weeks before an upcoming solstice or equinox.

- Pick the remaining fruit before the weather turns too cold or too hot and ripen them indoors.

STEP 7

Large Fruit

I began running, I mean jogging, long-distance when I was in college. I started the summer after my sophomore year by heading to the end of the block, walking, and then jogging to the end of the next block and walking again. Slowly but surely, I was able to jog longer, and by the end of the summer, I could manage a 5K. But it wasn't until my senior year in college that I attempted a half-marathon, on a racecourse I made up myself.

I jogged a six-mile route routinely, so I knew all I had to do was double the distance and I'd be there. Simple enough, right?

So I took off, just me and my running shoes. More than two hours later, I arrived back at my campus barely breathing and with tears in my eyes. I had finished, but running double the distance felt like it took a lot more than twice as much effort.

Successfully growing your first large-fruiting plants is kind of like finishing a half-marathon.

You're going to need lots of space, lots of time, lots of water, and lots of snacks! These plants require forethought and planning. There are a lot of steps between the start and the finish lines.

Even though it's a long journey, growing large fruit is also really fun.

It may be more than 3, even 4, months before you get your first juicy bite. But those tears in your eyes? It's because your first harvest is really that good.

Here's the good news: even though they need more space, time, and sunshine, the tending may not be as tedious as what you saw in Step 6 of your garden journey. Good thing, because each plant

at this step will be growing for quite a while. Daily tending needs would likely wear you out long before the race is over.

In this section you'll learn about large bush plants, large vining plants, and even a few perennial berry plants. We won't step into fruit trees in this book, but we'll come close by exploring berry plants you can grow right alongside your kitchen garden.

Plant Families

You've met many plant families in your climb so far. Now that we're nearing the top step, we reacquaint ourselves with old friends and meet one new plant family.

Cucurbitaceae. Many of the large-fruiting plants belong in the cucurbit family, including gourds and melons. If you're imagining growing a pumpkin patch in your very own backyard, wiping garden-fresh watermelon juice from your chin at the end of summer, or placing a centerpiece of homegrown gourds on your table for winter decor, you're in the right place.

Of course, cucumbers, squash, and zucchini—plants from Step 6—are also in this family, but they finish producing early enough to qualify as small fruit.

Brassicaceae. Technical gardeners out there will shake their finger at me for placing broccoli and Brussels sprouts in the large-fruit category, but let me explain.

If we're talking plant parts, broccoli, cauliflower, Romanesco, and Brussels sprouts are technically flower buds, not fruit. That being said, many take more than 100 days to form and share the same space and tending needs as larger-fruiting plants. So forgive me as I place flower buds in a fruiting category. Trust me: it works.

Rosaceae. Finally, we meet a plant family that includes foods that people call fruit! The rose family includes strawberries, blueberries, blackberries, and more. Unlike the other fruit we'll cover in this step, the berry cousins are perennials. These plants continue in your garden for many years, fruiting from new growth on the plant, grown from the same root, again and again. The setup for these plants is a little different from that of annual fruiting plants, but many of the practices still work.

Setup

SPACE

When Jason and I first met, we could fit all of our belongings (between the two of us) in one car. Now, 15 years later, with four kids and two dogs, we can't even fit all our family members into one car—it takes a minivan, and even then, the vehicle is packed!

We've grown up and out, and along the way, the space we occupy has too.

It's the same for the plants in Step 7. Many large-fruiting plants could grow to the size of our first car, even a minivan

ROMANESCO

BUTTERNUT SQUASH

RASPBERRIES

SMALL PUMPKINS

BRUSSELS SPROUTS

KABOCHA SQUASH

in some instances, so growing them in containers or raised beds is often not worth the effort.

In fact, I recommend planting almost all large-fruiting plants directly in the ground. Real estate in raised beds is just too precious to give to these sprawling plants that will want each and every inch of the garden. The easiest way to set up an in-ground row garden is to build on the soil you already have with a technique known as sheet mulching: Simply place a layer of cardboard over the existing soil or sod of the planting area, and then add a thick layer of compost, hay, chopped leaves, and shredded paper that will break down over time. Top off each row with at least 3 inches of compost, and then plant into the sheet-mulched bed.

When planting in an in-ground row garden like this, I recommend following

LARGE-FRUIT FAMILIES AT A GLANCE

FAMILY	COMMON PLANTS	GROWTH HABIT
Brassicaceae	Broccoli, cauliflower, Romanesco, Brussels sprouts	Bush
Cucurbitaceae	Melons, pumpkins, gourds	Vine
Rosaceae	Strawberries, blueberries, raspberries, blackberries	Bush and vine
Solanaceae	Large eggplants, tomatillos	Bush and vine

the plant-spacing rules on the back of seed packets or purchased-plant labels.

If you read my first book, *Kitchen Garden Revival*, you'll know I boldly throw plant-spacing rules to the wind. You might even be thinking, *Wait, Nicole, you made me take a planting pledge to ignore these rules! Are you now telling me to obey them?*

As with any rule (or promise to break the rules), there are exceptions.

Planting intensively works in a raised-bed kitchen garden with trellises that grow crops vertically and in deep beds that make it possible for roots to grow down instead of horizontally. But plant-spacing rules (typically found on seed packets) do apply to row-garden setups—the type of planting I recommend for larger fruit, as they perform best when given the space to spread out. So this time, I'm giving you permission to follow the rules. But only this once, okay?

Though these plants do need more space, their tending needs aren't as demanding, nor are the harvests as frequent compared to smaller fruit, roots, and leaves. So it makes sense to grow them in rows rather than packing them into a tightly controlled space designed for your daily tending convenience.

Plant in 3-foot-wide rows or mounds that are an adequate distance from one another so the plants will have plenty of room to grow to maturity without blocking sunlight or bumping into one another.

Cucurbit plants like gourds, pumpkins, and melons can be planted either in mounds where each vine grows in opposing directions or in rows where each plant is allotted plenty of room to spread wide and long. Pumpkin seeds, for example, should be planted about 1 inch deep, only 3 to 5 seeds per mound. Once seedlings appear, thin them to 2 or

The Step-by-Step to Sheet Mulching

1 Lay cardboard or construction paper down in the garden space.

2 Cover with leaves.

3 Layer straw, shredded paper, or more leaves.

4 Top with finished compost.

5 Prepare to plant into the top-layer compost.

3 plants per mound. The seeds need to stay moist until they sprout, but they're not as fragile or as needy as leafy green or root crop seeds.

Planting in a mound keeps the soil warm and aids in germination, but pumpkins can also be planted in rows. If planting in a row, space seeds 6 to 12 inches apart. Plan accordingly, as pumpkins need lots of space to grow.

Plants in the brassica family do great in rows too, as each plant grows in a bush-like shape that can become 3 to 4 feet wide. Brussels sprouts plants, for instance, get transplanted to your garden after being started indoors and should be spaced 2 feet apart in rows set 3 feet apart.

Fruit bushes and plants can be planted in rows as well, with strawberry plants growing 1 per square foot, raspberry and blueberry bushes 1 every 2 square feet, and upright blackberries 1 every 3 square feet.

For both berry plants and cucurbits like gourds and melons, you can still use trellises or vertical supports, even when you're growing in the ground, to enable the plants to spread out vertically, make the most of your growing space, and promote healthier plants. Cattle panel, rebar, or simply stakes and string are often used for support instead of more ornamental trellises due to the larger growing space.

SUNLIGHT

Once I'd officially "mastered" my raised-bed kitchen garden, I was ready for a new challenge. After seeing my neighbor's success with a backyard pumpkin patch the previous year, I figured I would try it too. I was already imagining the kids and me picking our autumn pumpkins from the backyard. So I did what any naïve gardener would do and ordered about 5 yards of compost delivered to the driveway.

Let me explain: I had a load of cardboard boxes ready for recycling and a spot we'd recently cleared of old brush in the backyard. I was ready to use the sheet-mulching method and plant some pumpkin seeds.

A few wheelbarrows in, however, and it was clear that I overestimated my arm strength and underestimated the weight of compost.

It took all weekend but I did, in fact, set up a sheet-mulched garden plot, first covering the soil with cardboard and then adding layers and layers of compost. I followed the directions on the seed packets for spacing, made mounds for each type of pumpkin and gourd seed I planted, and topped it all off with proper plant labels.

Days passed, and things looked promising: there were tiny sprouts of green all over the patch. More days came and went, and the vines grew longer and longer until they sprawled over the entire area.

But as the long summer days began to shorten, I had loads of green vines and a few small bottleneck gourds in my pumpkin patch, but no sign of even one pumpkin. I was missing something, and that something was sunlight.

Our backyard is home to trees that are more than 30 years old, and their generous canopies mean spots in our yard get sun for a few hours at most. I might have had the space to level up to Step 7 in gardening, but the amount of available light should have kept me on Steps 2 through 5. Next time, it'll have to be a carrot patch.

Large-fruiting plants will absorb as much sunlight as you can give them for as long as you can give it to them. These plants do best in wide open spaces where

there's nothing to obstruct the light. This is why so many of them are truly farm plants. These plants often require an open field without homes or trees that block even a minute of summer sun.

At a minimum, large-fruiting plants need 8 hours of sunlight a day, and they'll thrive when they receive 10 to 12+ hours of sun. If you've got shady spots with fewer than 8 hours of direct sun, you might want to skip this step. Or maybe try growing a few to test your location before going big with 5 yards of compost and a full pumpkin patch.

SEASON

Except for brassica family members, large-fruiting plants do not tolerate frost. That means they can't go outside before the final frost date of the cool season.

You might be thinking, *Then I'll start them outside once it's warm.*

Here's the catch: most of these large-fruiting plants also require at least 100 days to complete their fruiting process before the end of the warm season. So if your region's warm seasons don't last 100 days at a time, you'll need to give your plants a 30- to 45-day head start. To do this, start seeds indoors during the cooler season and transplant them outside when the weather warms.

Gourds, pumpkins, and melons all require the heat of summer to complete their growing stages. Start gourds and melons by seed under grow lights 4 to 6 weeks before your last frost date. Pumpkins can be started indoors 3 weeks before the last frost date. These larger cucurbits need to be in the warm soil for

SPACING GUIDELINES FOR LARGE-FRUIT PLANTS

PLANT	SPACE AT PLANTING
Blackberries	1 per 3 square feet
Blueberries	1 per 2 square feet
Brassicas	1 per 2–3 square feet
Eggplants (large)	1 per 2–3 square feet
Gourds	1 per square foot
Melons	1 per square foot
Pumpkins	1–2 per square foot
Raspberries	1 per 2 square feet
Strawberries	1 per square foot

90 to 120 (maybe even 150) days before the fruit reaches full maturity.

Perennial berry bushes can be planted in early spring or fall. They need time to develop strong roots before winter and then will begin producing new canes and stems as soon as the ground thaws. They finish their berry production before temperatures begin to drop once more.

Plants in the brassica family are the only ones in Step 7 that can withstand frost. Broccoli, cauliflower, and Brussels sprouts actually prefer cooler weather. They'll need at least 90 to 100 days of temps between 45 and 85°F to complete their growth, so again, it's a good idea to start brassica seeds indoors about 30 days before the soil is warm enough to set the transplants in rows.

Care

WATER

It was one of the cutest things: my children, each one clutching a few seeds, standing by their own little mound of soil and planting their first watermelons.

The day they pushed their seeds into the soil, they were already picturing the juice of their first delicious harvests dribbling down their chins (or maybe it was me planning the picture?). They weren't prepared for what came next. Thirty, 50, 75 days in, the hot days of summer continued and the promising watermelon vines grew less green and more brown with each day. I'm not sure my kids were paying attention, but those neglected melons taught me a valuable lesson: it's hard to get something out of a plant that you didn't put in. Without enough water, you won't get a watermelon, at least not one you want to eat. I never got that picture.

In the first seven steps of the LRF system, most garden plants need 1 inch of water per week. But you'll need to multiply that number for large-fruiting plants, which require 1 inch of water *for each square foot of plant growth*. Can you do the math? This means that for one large melon plant that takes up 10 square feet, you need to provide the plant with 10 inches of water per week to meet that plant's needs. They don't call it watermelon for nothing.

When watering these plants, be sure the water reaches the roots, not the leaves. Larger-fruiting plants will have

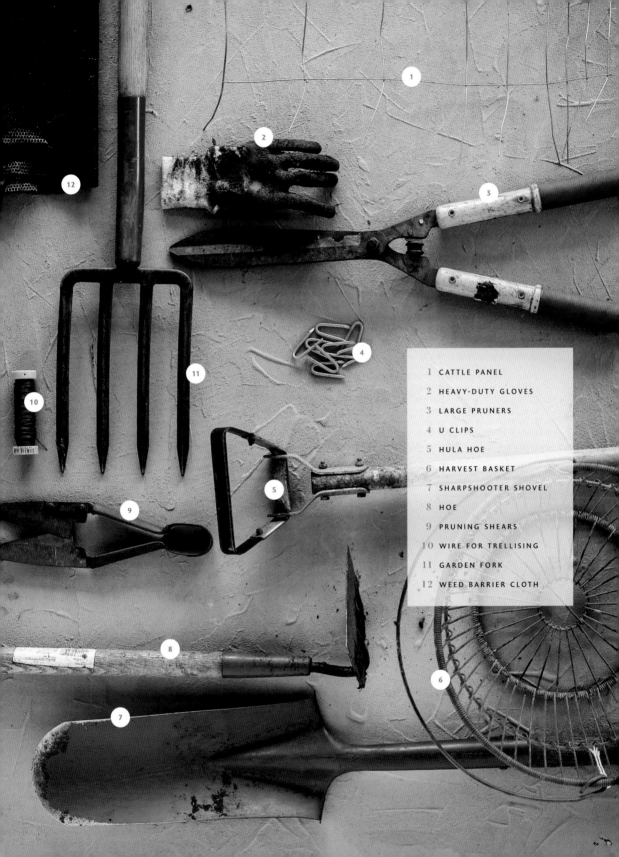

1 CATTLE PANEL

2 HEAVY-DUTY GLOVES

3 LARGE PRUNERS

4 U CLIPS

5 HULA HOE

6 HARVEST BASKET

7 SHARPSHOOTER SHOVEL

8 HOE

9 PRUNING SHEARS

10 WIRE FOR TRELLISING

11 GARDEN FORK

12 WEED BARRIER CLOTH

deeper root systems that can reach down and get water when they start to run dry. For melons and gourds, once you've reached day 100, start watering less. Then halt watering altogether the final 1 to 2 weeks before harvesting. This allows the inside of the fruit to become sweeter while the flesh stays nice and crisp for harvest.

NUTRIENTS

As you grow large-fruiting plants, you'll laugh at your former self who thought it was a lot of work to rinse sprouts or add a little compost to the salad garden. These fruiting plants are like teenagers—they grow in their sleep and wake up *starving.*

You'll follow a weekly or biweekly feeding schedule similar to the one you used for small-fruiting plants, but now you'll pay closer attention to the nutrients the plant may be missing at each growth stage.

The best way to care for large-fruiting plants is to start strong. Adding more nutrition to the soil and plants later in the season won't make up for a slow beginning, so take the time to set up a nutrient-rich soil when you plant.

Large brassica plants do best with a pH around 6.8. Use a rich compost to amend the soil before planting. Be careful not to add too much nitrogen-rich material to these plants, or you'll end up with lots of leaves and fewer of the flowering heads you're hoping to harvest.

Gourds, pumpkins, and melons are considered "heavy feeders." They grow best in compost-rich soil that's been amended with organic fertilizer. Add as much as 1 cup of organic fertilizer below the transplant or seed on the day you plant these cucurbits.

Almost all large plants will eat up most of the soil nutrients within the first month. Since these plants still have months of growth to go, it's important to add more nutrients to the soil regularly. Use a nitrogen-rich fertilizer in their first month of growing, and then switch to a potassium- and phosphorus-rich one once the plant starts flowering and fruiting. I recommend fish- or kelp-based fertilizers for later-stage fertilizing.

Slow the fertilization process as harvest time draws closer. When your fruit is 1 to 2 weeks away from harvest, stop adding fertilizers so the plant can store its nutrients, sweeten its fruit, and be ready to pick.

The Step-by-Step to Planting Large Gourds

1 Gather seeds, a watering can, a plant tag, a hula or stirrup hoe, and extra compost.

2 Use the hula hoe to turn the top layer of soil.

3 Add fresh compost and mound it.

4 Plant seeds 6 inches to 1 foot apart on the mound.

5 Water in well.

6 Label the mound with a plant tag for easy identification.

TENDING

You can increase the likelihood of getting more fruit by performing certain tending chores: in particular, protecting, supporting, pruning, and weeding.

The best way to protect large-fruiting plants is by covering them with frost cloth at the beginning of their growth, gardener's micromesh fabric during their early months in the garden, and shade cloth on the hottest days of summer if temperatures rise too high. Floating row covers put in place from the day you

transplant your seedlings outdoors will discourage pests like cucumber beetles and squash vine borers, but remove the covers once flowers begin to appear to give pollinators access to the plants.

Large-fruiting plants that sprawl along the ground don't need extra support, but Brussels sprouts, broccoli, and Romanesco can become top-heavy. Use a stake to support each plant as it matures. All fruiting plants benefit from hilling: adding fresh finished compost around the base to support the plants once they have grown their first few sets of leaves.

If you choose to trellis blackberries or gourds, check the vines weekly to be sure they're still connected to the trellis, and tie up vines that need help attaching.

Pruning can direct more energy to growing larger fruit. If you choose to prune, remove the small vines that grow laterally on gourds and pumpkins. Large eggplants can be pruned by keeping the plant to one main stem as it starts to mature and cutting away nonfruiting stems. Berries need special types of pruning. Raspberry and blackberry canes should be cut back once a year, cutting only the canes that fruited the year prior. Strawberry runners (stems that extend from the main plant to form a new root and plant system) should be pruned away and replanted each year as well.

Because large vines and bushy plants grow for an extended length of time, maintaining airflow in and around the plants is a must to prevent mold and powdery mildew. Be sure berry vines are

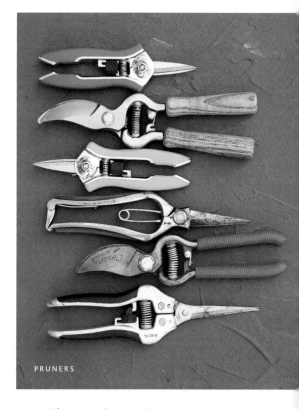

PRUNERS

spaced far enough apart that each one receives ample sunlight and fresh air. Do the same for vining gourds, melons, and pumpkins by trying to avoid vines crossing and tangling (at least at the beginning). Every week or two, gently lift and turn any gourds and melons that rest on the ground to prevent rotting. Finally, for brassicas like broccoli and cauliflower, prune back excess leaves to maintain distance between the plants for optimal ventilation and sun.

The final tending tasks for large-fruiting plants involve weeding and mulching. Because these plants are in the ground, you'll need to weed around them often to keep competition away. While most

PLANT	FRUITS PER PLANT
Berries	10–20 pounds
Broccoli/cauliflower	1, plus side shoots
Brussels sprouts	10–15
Eggplants (large)	4–6
Gourds	2–3
Melons	2–4
Pumpkins	2–5
Strawberries	5–7

gardeners encourage the use of wood chips or leaf mulch in the garden, I've found it to be an effective hiding place for plant pests. Yes, mulch reduces weeds and retains soil moisture, but it's also the perfect camouflage for critters of all sorts. I recommend using compost to retain moisture and nutrients in the garden instead of wood chips or leaves. And if you'd like to add mulch, I'd use pine straw instead of wood chips if it's locally available.

Harvest

TIME

Larger-fruiting plants will take at least 100 days to fruit from planting by seed. So go in with a plan for how long these plants need to stay in their space, how often they need watering or tending, and when they'll be ready for the big harvest.

Brassica plants grow for 100 days or longer. Large cucurbits like gourds, pumpkins, and melons, plus eggplants from the Solanaceae family, will spend 4 to 6 months in the garden.

Perennial berry plants live in the garden year-round but actively produce stems, then leaves, and finally flowers and fruit over a 90- to 120-day period. Strawberries fruit first, then blueberries and raspberries, and finally blackberries after the warmest days of summer.

Running this race is a time commitment, but you don't have to keep a sprinter's pace the whole way. In fact, you'll find that over the growing season, it's the plants that are doing all the hard work. It seems like the longer we wait for something, the sweeter it tastes, and like a big meal after exercise, the fruit you pick will truly be a trophy for your efforts.

PRODUCTION

You've waited as long as 4, 5, even 6 months for this day, and it's finally time to harvest. Grab your pruners and wheelbarrow (these crops aren't going to fit in a basket!).

But wait—how will you know if your plant is ready to harvest?

Even though your plants can't talk (at least not in your language), each large-fruiting plant has a sign to tell you when it's ready to be picked.

Melons seem to have a special way to say, "I'm ready!" A melon's netting pattern, for example, will become more visible, and a crack will appear at the base of the stem. The color deepens and becomes richer too. Tendrils drying around the fruit are yet another sign that the fruit is about ready to pick. A final

readiness test is to check the feel of the skin on the fruit. Does it feel tight but give a little when you press it with your thumb? Then tap the melon. Does it sound hollow? If so, it's ready.

One or two weeks before harvesting gourds, pumpkins, and melons, stop watering and fertilizing the plants. When you harvest, include at least 3 to 4 inches of the main stem to keep with the fruit as you store it.

Ripening brassicas like broccoli and cauliflower form a tight flower cluster that swells larger daily. This happens over a period of weeks, and you can harvest

at any point in this progression. The trick is waiting long enough to get a good harvest but not so long that the florets turn yellow and burst into flowers. Once this happens, although the plant is still edible, the flavor will be different from what you expect.

For some brassica plants, particularly broccoli, you can cut at the base of the floret and leave the main plant to keep growing. If weather conditions remain optimal, the plant produces side shoots that you can add to your harvest basket in a matter of weeks.

Some larger fruit tastes better if picked after the first frost. This includes Brussels sprouts, broccoli, Romanesco, and gourds. Other fruit like berries and melons should be harvested before frost arrives. For brassicas, only pick as many as you need. Sprouts can stay on the stem through the first weeks of winter, even after first frost.

Taking This Step

You've made it to Step 7. Let's take a moment to consider this milestone.

While you wait for your pumpkin to grow and grow and grow some more, you can harvest microgreens, herbs, salad leaves, radishes, beets, potatoes, carrots, beans, peppers, and tomatoes. All these plants are growing together; some will be available to harvest today, some will need pruning, some will be ready in a few weeks, and others will need months more in the garden. Together, the leaves, roots,

and all sizes of fruit keep our plates full and our bodies nourished.

Those first few steps you took in your gardening journey were important to get you to this step, but you absolutely can (and should) continue to grow plants at each step you've taken to get here, all at the same time.

So yes, it can be quite a long time before you'll be able to harvest your larger fruit, but you won't be sitting with an empty plate while you wait.

Growing Larger Fruit

SET UP

- Use the sheet-mulching method to convert land to growing space by leveling the space, laying down cardboard, and adding inches of compost-amended soil.

- Gather the seeds, transplants, or bare-root plants.

- Use tags and mark the areas for each plant.

- Add nitrogen-rich fertilizer to the bottom of each planting hill or row.

PLANT

- Create hills of compost-amended soil or pure compost.

- Plant 1 to 3 melon, gourd, or pumpkin seeds per hill.

- Transplant broccoli, cauliflower, and other large brassicas in rows spaced 3 feet apart.

- Plant large eggplants in a raised bed with 2 to 3 square feet of space.

- Plant young or bare-root berry plants in a slightly raised bed or in amended soil next to a supporting trellis (for all but strawberries).

- Water in the plants well over the first 2 weeks.

TEND

- Water at least 1 inch per week or 1 gallon for every square foot of gourd, melon, and pumpkin plants as well as large eggplants.

- Fertilize with organic potassium and phosphorus sources every 1 or 2 weeks once flowering and fruiting begin.

- Prune away vines that cross or tangle with other vines.

- Maintain good airflow between plants.

- Turn melons and gourds regularly to prevent rot.

HARVEST

- Check the fruit for signs of ripeness.

- Test one fruit from each plant and then proceed to harvest as needed.

- Complete harvesting before frost for melons, berries, and eggplants.

- Wait until after the first frost for brassica plants, gourds, and pumpkins.

Seeds

At the end of a good story, you're back at the beginning, often with the same hero who's been on a long journey and grown along the way. Now at Step 8, you've arrived at the end of your own garden story, and you're definitely a hero. But your plants are the star of the show, because the one seed you began with has turned into hundreds if not thousands more.

You can grow any plant for its seeds. In fact, I grow seeds every year, even when I don't intend to do so.

Lettuces and greens often bolt and go to seed in the garden, peppers or tomatoes may split and leave their seeds in the soil, and herbs flower on their own and produce hundreds of seeds each season.

But in this chapter, the focus is primarily on plants that are grown specifically for the consumption, not just the saving, of their seed.

Plant Families

In this step, we'll focus on just a few plant families grown for their seed, but know that there are lots more to choose from. Most seed-producing crops require a lot of space, which is out of reach for many home gardeners. Our focus here will be on plants that can be grown within a fairly small footprint.

Fabaceae. One of the key plant families for growing seeds is the legume family, which includes some peas in the cool season and other peas and beans in the warm and hot seasons. You met this family in Step 6 if you grew peas for the fresh green pods. Now you're growing these plants for dried seeds instead.

Gramineae. This family includes corn, wheat, rye, barley, and maize. Imagine tall plants that hold themselves upright and produce clusters of flowers and seeds along their strong main stem. This plant family produces much, if not all, of the grains we enjoy in the kitchen and in our cereal bowl.

Asteraceae. The aster family includes sunflowers and other flowers grown for seeds. You may recall this family from Step 3, since it houses many of the delicious greens that end up in your salad bowl.

Again, there are many other seeds you can grow, but we'll focus on these as they're the simplest to plant in the home garden.

Setup

SPACE

That first summer we planted our garden (remember, the one with the tomatoes?), we bought anything that looked interesting at the plant shop, including corn seeds. We loved corn from the farmers market, and they always had so many ears piled up on the tables . . . Surely it would be easy to grow some ourselves. We planted one packet of seeds in a few rows alongside our potatoes and beans. We weren't going to need to grocery shop soon (at least that's what we told ourselves).

The corn sprang up quickly and looked promising—until the weather report promised us big thunderstorms and a possible tornado. We spent the day sheltering inside. The next morning we headed out to check on our little garden. The beans were hanging on; the potatoes were still growing. But the corn? It was lying down on the job, completely flattened by the previous day's winds.

We did our best to resurrect the plants, but a quick search online and a few gardening books for reference later, we realized our problem wasn't the wind. It was the way we'd planted the corn.

SEED FAMILIES AT A GLANCE

FAMILY	COMMON PLANTS
Asteraceae	Sunflowers
Fabaceae	Beans, peas
Gramineae	Corn, wheat, rye, barley, maize

These plants need support, not from us but from one another. Instead of a few plants, we should've planted dozens. Instead of a few rows, we needed *lots*. Corn is one of those crops you can't just "experiment with." It's a go-big-or-don't-go kind of situation.

We pulled the plants, our lesson learned, and headed back to the farmers market.

Beans and peas are the exception here, but many of the grains and seeds you'll grow in this step need a more complex setup, more space, and more commitment than plants from the other steps.

I recommend you grow seed crops other than beans and peas outside your raised beds, in a row garden. These plants will occupy the garden space for quite a long time, and they'll grow to become tall, towering plants, making them more difficult to access and reach when in a raised garden.

And because you're growing them for their seeds, it's a good idea to grow each type of plant alone, in its own section of the garden, so you don't risk cross-pollination of plant varieties. Grains, especially corn, need to be planted alongside other plants of the same variety with at least 12 rows of plants together to ensure proper pollination.

Plant beans and peas in rows in a raised bed or row garden in loose soil that's been amended with compost. To speed up the germination process, soak your seeds overnight (but no longer) before planting. Since beans and peas require only a little bit of space for each plant, seeds can be spaced 4 inches apart in rows 6 inches apart if in a raised garden bed. If your peas and beans are the pole or vining variety, plant the seeds a little closer together along a trellis or plant support. Keep in mind that to get harvests you can enjoy regularly on your plate, you'll need quite a few plants (as many as 30 per person).

For sunflowers and other flowering seeds, plant seeds directly in the ground in rows 6 inches apart. If you've ever looked at a seed catalog, you know there are at least a thousand varieties of sunflowers you can grow, ranging from

The Step-by-Step to Growing Peas

1 Gather a trellis, seeds, a dibber, and a watering can.

2 Install the trellis securely at least 1 foot into the ground.

3 Use a dibber to drill holes to 1 to 2 inches in depth.

4 Plant one seed per hole near the trellis supports.

5 Water in.

6 Check for good seed–soil contact and be sure the seeds stay buried.

small to *huge*. Once you know the variety you're growing, take the size of the mature flower and double it—that should be the minimum distance between each seed you plant.

For corn and other grains, use the sheet-mulching method (page 198) to create a garden space, then dig trenches about 4 inches deep in rows 4 inches apart. Each seed can be planted every 4 inches in the trenches. If you drive past a field of corn, you'll notice how tightly packed the plants actually are. So much so that it's often difficult to see through the field once the plants grow to full maturity. If in a few months you find yourself standing in the middle of rows and rows of closely planted corn, unable to see anything but the corn stalk in front of you, you did it right.

SUNLIGHT

Seeds love sunlight, and lots of it.

When I moved to Chicago, I started to understand why most of America's grains and seeds are grown in the Midwest. Around the summer solstice, Chicago mornings start as early as 4:30 with the birds spotting the sun on the horizon, and the day doesn't end until almost 9:00 P.M. All this and I'm not even in the northernmost part of the country.

Summer is filled with sun all day, nearly every day, and endless plains, which make for boring hikes but wonderful places to grow seeds.

Take a lesson from the farmers in the Midwest and search for the sunniest and flattest spot in your landscape to grow seeds. Your plants will be happiest with at least 10 hours per day. Think of *Little House on the Prairie* and search for the place with few structures nearby—such as trees, other homes, or tall fences. Your ideal is a spot where these plants will absorb every minute of sunlight the day produces for many stretches of days together.

SEASON

Besides peas, most of the plants you grow for their seeds will be planted after your last frost date and will grow through the entirety of the warmest growing months of the year. Your seed harvests (again, apart from peas) will take place at the end of the warm season just as the weather returns to cool-season status.

Peas in the Fabaceae family love growing in the cooler parts of the year, meaning peas will grow and flourish on either side of your warm season(s). Most pea seeds can be planted as soon as the soil can be worked and then again as early as 60 days before the last frost.

Plan on planting 1 bush pea plant every few inches in rows in the cool seasons of the year. You can give that space over to bush beans in the warm season and then lima beans or crowder peas in the hot season (if you have one).

While sunflowers and beans, plus corn, maize, and other grains can be started before the threat of frost passes, these plants are not tolerant of extreme freezing temperatures. It's best to wait to plant until the threat of frost has passed unless you can cover the sprouts to protect them from frost and snow.

Care

WATER

By this step, the seeds we're growing to produce more seeds tend to be larger than other varieties, so soak bean, pea, and corn seeds in water overnight to help break down the seed coat so the seed starts growing its roots and shoots sooner.

Once planted, seed-bearing plants must have a consistent watering schedule. This is especially critical in the first 2 weeks of growth. After the plants are established, devise a watering system that ensures each plant receives 1 to 2 inches of water per week, including rainwater.

When the plants are nearing maturity and seeds will soon be ready to harvest, slow the watering schedule to allow the seeds to finish maturing without too much moisture.

NUTRIENTS

When growing plants for their seeds, start with the healthiest soil possible. Take time to amend the soil before planting seeds. Follow the nutrient needs for plants as described in the small-fruiting stage (see page 178), adding nitrogen in the leaf-growing stage and then supplementing with phosphorus and potassium

this time. Her answer? "Honey, if the caterpillars don't want to eat it, you shouldn't either."

This was a new perspective. It took me a minute to realize she had a point. And with that, I grabbed my bag and filled it with more corn, not at all worried about the caterpillars and eager to go home and feast.

Take it from my farmers market friend: if you've got pests on your crops, it can be a good sign. Your plants are so delicious and organic that everybody wants a bite.

Pest issues aside, the one area where seed plants are less demanding is in their tending needs. These are mostly field plants that are often planted all at once, tended all at once, and harvested all at once. The upshot: unlike the herbs you snip from weekly, the greens you clean and harvest every few days, or the fruiting crops you prune, fertilize, and trellis, seed plants are mostly plant-it-and-forget-it.

So if you have the space and sunlight, and you don't mind the long wait, growing plants for their seeds can be an extremely rewarding experience.

Apart from watering and fertilizing a bit, the few tending chores necessary are to support the plants and tend to pests.

The first way to support these plants is to hill them. Pushing a little additional compost or rich garden soil along the stem area of the plants supports their growth, encourages more root formation, and keeps your plants from falling over like mine did during that storm.

to grow strong roots and create healthy flowers. After the flowers form or the fruit has been set, there's no need to add more nutrients to the soil. At this point, the goal is for the plant to finish its life cycle and fully form healthy and nutrient-rich seeds.

TENDING

I was a little shocked one day to open up an ear of corn from the farmers market and find tiny caterpillars crawling around the yellow kernels I was so eager to eat. Surprised, yes, but not so disgusted that I threw it out. I still boiled it up and dug in.

The next week, when I circled back to the same market stall, I asked if the vendor could help me be certain the cobs I purchased didn't have little critters

For some taller grain crops and for vining plants like pole beans, you can support the plants by securing them to trellises or poles. Simply stroll through the garden every few weeks to ensure the vines have all the support they need as they keep reaching for the sunlight.

Finally, playing garden inspector can ensure your seed-growing plants make it to the end of the race. Pests like caterpillars, aphids, and flies love to attack young green plants at the beginning of their growth. And you might be competing with birds and other wildlife for the nutritious seeds you've waited so long to harvest at the end of the season. Be watchful and take action immediately when needed.

The simplest way to protect your crops, both at the beginning and the end of their life cycle, is by setting up garden mesh. There's nothing better or more secure than a physical barrier to keep pests from getting to the seed crop before you do.

You can also use garlic barrier (an extract of garlic mixed with water and sprayed on plants) or insecticidal soap to fight off pests that like to linger on plants' stems and leaves.

As always, the best pest control is your own shadow. Even though these plants may look like they've got this on their own from afar, step in and take a closer look every week to be sure there's no small critter hiding in your grain crops.

Harvest

TIME

Plants take quite a while to complete their journey from seed to seed. The process may be certain, but it isn't quick.

Peas and beans in the Fabaceae family require the least amount of time, generally completing their growing cycle and producing mature pea pods and seeds in 60 to 75 days.

Sunflowers and other flowers grown for their seeds need at least 100 days before they're ready to harvest, although you get to enjoy their flowers many days before that.

"Knee-high by the Fourth of July" is a common saying among corn farmers. Essentially, these plants must be well established and growing quickly just weeks after summer solstice. Corn, maize, and other grains require as many as 120 days to complete their growing cycle and even longer if the goal is to harvest dried seeds.

As soon as you plant your seeds, mark the calendar for 100 to 120 days from planting and then start envisioning the moment when you'll harvest and enjoy the end of this long story.

PRODUCTION

The children's book *One Grain of Rice* tells the story of how a smart young girl won over a king's entire estate by asking for just 1 grain of rice that would double every day for 30 days. In the beginning, the king laughs as just 1, then 2, then 4 grains of rice leave his property. But by day 30, when 536,870,912 grains of rice are taken away, it's the smart little girl, and the entire kingdom she shares with, doing all the laughing.

As you grow your own seeds, you will learn the power of doubling too.

One seed of corn can produce 2 to 4 ears of corn. But here's the magic: 1 ear of corn holds about 800 seeds. Essentially, 1 becomes as many as 3,200 more!

One pea seed can produce at least 20 to 30 pods per plant during the cool season, and each pod holds 4 to 6 peas. That's 1 pea growing into 180 more peas. Beans are similar, with 1 bean seed capable of growing about 20 pods per plant and each pod holding about 6 beans. One becomes 120.

Seed Focus: Sunflowers

Before planting sunflowers, amend your soil with compost and set up rows for planting seeds after all chance of frost has passed. Use high-quality sunflower seeds and bury them just 1 inch below the soil surface. Cover your seeds with 1 inch of compost-amended soil and then water in thoroughly.

Watch for sprouts within 7 days of planting. Continue to give your plants at least 1 inch of water per week, applying it at the root.

When your first sunflower forms, celebrate! Then fertilize with a phosphorus-rich organic fertilizer. Cut the first flowers to encourage maximum output later. Once enough flowers have formed, leave the flower heads to keep growing.

As the flowers begin to wilt and dry, cover each flower head with mesh fabric or a bag to protect the seeds from birds. Wait for these seeds to dry out before cutting each stem and bringing the seed heads to store indoors. After a few weeks, rake the seeds from each seed head and store them in a cool, dry spot.

Depending on the sunflower variety, 1 plant (that's a single sunflower head) can produce 1,000 to 2,000 seeds.

The numbers are impressive, but of course, you must remember what we're growing here. We've come back to the place where we began. Seeds, tiny promises we can hold in our hand. Nothing reminds you of both the magic and the frailty of the garden quite like holding a handful of seeds it took you months to grow. So much can grow from so little, and yet it'll take many plants to fill your plate.

To grow enough corn for yourself, you need to plant 10 to 15 plants. To grow enough beans, you'd need 30 plants. And if sunflower seeds are to replace your potato chip habit, you might need an entire field.

But even if you grow just enough for a few meals, one snack, or a single dish every week, you'll still be amazed at how one tiny seed can settle into the soil, swell until it bursts, and harness the sun's rays day after day after day before finally exploding into hundreds more of itself, perfect copies, all bundled together in a perfect arrangement that looks like a masterpiece.

Taking This Step

Seeds are truly one of the most magical things our planet holds. Your hands may never feel more full than when you're holding seeds you've grown yourself.

This is the final step to learning to grow in the kitchen garden.

It may sound cheesy, but doesn't this return to the beginning remind you of the song that never ends?

"It goes on and on, my friend. Some people started singing it, not knowing what it was. And we'll continue singing it forever just because."

This is the song of seed to sprout to leaves, roots, fruit, and back to seeds that the earth sings. Who knows how it all started, and who knows how it will end? But isn't it wonderful that we get to be part of this beautiful cycle in the garden?

Now that you know the steps to grow, you get to decide which step you'll take next.

Growing Seeds

SET UP

- Amend the soil with compost in rows or raised beds.
- Add nitrogen-rich fertilizer before planting.

PLANT

- Soak seeds in water overnight before planting.
- Plant seeds no more than twice their width deep and in tight rows or along trellis supports.
- Water in well.

TEND

- Water regularly at least 1 to 2 inches per week.
- Weed the area around the plants.
- Provide supports if needed.
- Fertilize with potassium and phosphorus until the plants have finished flowering.

HARVEST

- Leave the seeds to fully form on the plant.
- Protect the seeds with physical barriers if pests are present.
- Stop additional watering or fertilizing at least 2 weeks before harvest.
- Ensure that the seeds are at optimal stage before harvesting.
- Fully dry the seeds or seedpods before storing.

Take the Next Step

What stands between you and a garden-centered life?

Is it years of experience, a big plot of land, or a green thumb?

If you think something is standing between you and that garden you've been dreaming about, you're right.

But it's just the fact that you haven't had a system to follow.

And this system is just a few steps. Eight steps, to be exact. And as soon as you start climbing, you are on your way to making the garden part of your everyday.

Few of us want gradual these days. We're impatient!

It's true: some things are good when they happen fast.

But learning to garden isn't one of them.

It's taken thousands of years for humans to figure out how to grow plants, how to cultivate the varieties that grow best for us, how to give each plant what it needs so that it grows as well, or better, under our watch than it would in the wild.

And I thought I could just purchase a pot from the store and end up with tomatoes!

The process for learning and growing with your garden matters. You'll grow up as your garden does. You'll dig deeper when you pull up those roots. You'll mature as your fruit gets sweeter.

The old saying "Give a man a fish and you feed him for a day . . ." applies here. Beginner's luck in the garden or immediate gratification is fun in the moment, but you miss the magic of knowing how to make it happen again (and again).

Now that you've made it this far, you know *how* to garden. You've got a system.

All that's missing is all the moments in between—the ones you'll have with your plants season after season. Each time, you'll either have success or a lesson that will make you more successful next time. You're now officially a gardener, and you will always know how to grow the next thing in your own garden, and not one season (or plant) can change that.

The Giving Garden

A favorite read-aloud is Shel Silverstein's *The Giving Tree*. In the book, there's a boy and an apple tree. The boy and the tree love each other from the start, and the boy enjoys every single part of the tree—he sits in the shade of the leaves, he hangs from the branches, and, of course, he eats the delicious apples.

The tree gets joy from watching the boy enjoy himself.

But as the boy grows older, he becomes greedy. First he wants all the apples to make some money. Then he wants all the limbs to build a house. He cuts the trunk to make a boat to run away and finally returns, still unhappy, to just sit on the stump, the only part of the tree he's left behind.

Though my kids and I love the book, reading those words aloud each night is sobering.

The story shows there's something off in our relationship as humans with plants. We can easily get into the mode of asking our plants and our gardens what they can do for us, forgetting the most valuable thing is that they're here in the first place—staying and growing, often-times despite us.

These eight steps to gardening are really an old story of *The Giving Garden*, a reframing of our relationship with plants, a re-appreciation of every single stage of a plant's life. A reminder that when we slow down and pay attention, we not only ben-efit from each part of the plant but also grow alongside our plants in patience, admiration, and pure, simple joy.

Sure, the fruit is shiny and bright and so very sweet and juicy. But the shade of the leaves can be just as satisfying, and the support of the strong trunk is often more necessary.

So, too, with our gardens.

Don't worry: there will be fruit in your garden. But before, during, and after that, there will be sprouts and roots and stems, and there will be leaves, millions and millions of leaves.

At every stage of its growth, the garden is giving, giving you little bites and tastes of its goodness. And this slow growth and progress is just what you need as a gardener—not everything all at once, but progress one day at a time.

Ask not what your garden can do for you. Instead, realize it's already done so much. Now all you've got to do is find your footing on the next step and be happy with what's growing right in front of you.

When you look up, I'll be there beside you, savoring my sprouts, drying my herbs, digging for new roots, drowning in kale, and keeping the raccoons and squirrels off my tomatoes.

Thank you for taking this journey with me. The best part of this system? There's always a new season to take the next step and grow your self again.

Keep Growing

Now that you've read this book, it's time to dig in and start planting. Start on Step 1 or any step that best fits the resources you have available right now. Remember, you can be growing from each step all at once, go back a step, or start all over any time you wish. And if you'd like assistance along the way, you can find it at leavesrootsandfruit.com.

At gardenary.com, you can also find a Gardenary-certified consultant to help you design and set up your garden right the first time, plus get daily support from our membership Gardenary 365.

Once you're growing, we'd love to help you help others learn to grow too. You can learn more about becoming a Gardenary consultant at gardenary.com.

ACKNOWLEDGMENTS

This book wouldn't be possible without the love and hard work of so many:

Eric Kelley—no one makes the kitchen garden look as good as you can. Thank you for the thousands of photos, the many steps you took through mud and rain, and the loving work you did to make this book so beautiful.

The Rooted Garden Houston Team—the hard work you do to consult, design, and maintain our kitchen gardens makes all these stories and photos possible.

Rooted Garden Houston Clients—so many of these kitchen gardens and plants pictured in this book and the lessons I share here are due to hundreds of clients who've trusted us to create a kitchen garden space for them.

Katie and Matt Oglesby—Katie is a Gardenary consultant in Lake Geneva, Wisconsin, and her kitchen garden is pictured throughout this book. Her wisdom and prowess in the kitchen garden are truly inspiring, and much of this book wouldn't be possible without her. And the stairs were only possible because of Matt's carpentry skills!

The Gardenary team—so many thanks to our staff that supports our students,

our design service, and our readers and community, so we all never stop growing. A special thank you to Julie for the countless edits.

The Gardenary consultants around the world who are bringing the kitchen garden back through great consulting and service in their own towns and cities.

Our Gardenary students and members that grow with us every season inside our app and membership

The Hay House team—thank you to Patty, Lisa, Monica, Melanie, and especially Paula, my editor, for your patience and hard work on this project.

My husband—a huge thank you to Jason, who is the reason so many of these garden experiences and stories happened. I love the life we're growing together.

My children: Carolyn, Brennan, Rebekah, and Elaine—my hope for the years ahead and the reason I love being home. I'm so proud of you.

My sister, Joannah, and her unending friendship in every season.

Kris Carr—my mentor whose kind guidance helped me in developing this book and bringing it to the publisher.

ABOUT THE AUTHOR

Nicole Johnsey Burke, founder of Gardenary, Inc., is on a crusade to bring back the kitchen garden, make gardening a profitable profession again, and basically save the planet one garden at a time. After starting Gardenary in 2015 as a business that designs, installs, and maintains kitchen gardens in Houston, Texas, Nicole launched Gardenary as a tech company that's taught thousands of students how to garden and trained hundreds of gardeners to start their own garden consulting businesses. In 2019, Nicole launched the Gardenary platform, and in 2020, she published her breakthrough book, *Kitchen Garden Revival*.

Parents to four children, Nicole and her husband, Jason, began experimenting with backyard gardening a bit in Virginia and then full stop in Nashville, Tennessee, and Houston, Texas. As Nicole's success in the garden grew, so did her passion for getting everyone else to start growing a little of their own food.

Nicole's hope and dream is that by the time her children are grown, the kitchen garden will be an ordinary part of everyone's lives once again. While many people can feel overwhelmed or just give up at the thought of all the challenges our growing world faces, kitchen gardens are a positive step that everyone can make to create change for the better.

www.gardenary.com

ABOUT THE PHOTOGRAPHER

Eric Kelley was selected as one of the best photographers in the country by Harper's Bazaar and Martha Stewart Weddings. Eric travels internationally for some of the most stunning and beautiful weddings and events. Known for authentic and delightful imagery, Eric's work can be seen in publications including Martha Stewart Weddings, The Knot national magazine, Southern Weddings magazine, Weddings Unveiled magazine, Southern Living Weddings, Magnolia Rouge, Once Wed, Style Me Pretty, and many more. Eric's photography can also be found in Nicole Johnsey Burke's first book, *Kitchen Garden Revival*.

You can visit him at erickelley.com.

INDEX

Hay House Titles of Related Interest

YOU CAN HEAL YOUR LIFE, the movie, starring Louise Hay & Friends
(available as an online streaming video)
www.hayhouse.com/louise-movie

THE SHIFT, the movie,
starring Dr. Wayne W. Dyer
(available as an online streaming video)
www.hayhouse.com/the-shift-movie

***

CRAZY, SEXY KITCHEN: 150 Plant Empowered Recipes to Ignite a
Mouthwatering Revolution, by Kris Carr

FOOD BABE KITCHEN: More than 100 Delicious, Real Food Recipes to
Change Your Body and Your Life, by Vani Hari

HEALING ADAPTOGENS: The Definitive Guide to Using Super Herbs and Mushrooms
for Your Body's Restoration, Defense, and Performance,
by Tero Isokauppila and Danielle Ryan Broida

WILD REMEDIES: How to Forage Healing Foods and Craft Your
Own Herbal Medicine, by Rosalee de la Foret & Emily Han

All of the above are available at your local bookstore,
or may be ordered by contacting Hay House (see next page).

***

We hope you enjoyed this Hay House book. If you'd like to receive our online catalog featuring additional information on Hay House books and products, or if you'd like to find out more about the Hay Foundation, please contact:

Hay House, Inc., P.O. Box 5100, Carlsbad, CA 92018-5100
(760) 431-7695 or (800) 654-5126
(760) 431-6948 (fax) or (800) 650-5115 (fax)
www.hayhouse.com® • www.hayfoundation.org

———

Published in Australia by: Hay House Australia Pty. Ltd.,
18/36 Ralph St., Alexandria NSW 2015
Phone: 612-9669-4299 • *Fax:* 612-9669-4144
www.hayhouse.com.au

Published in the United Kingdom by: Hay House UK, Ltd.,
The Sixth Floor, Watson House, 54 Baker Street, London W1U 7BU
Phone: +44 (0)20 3927 7290 • *Fax:* +44 (0)20 3927 7291
www.hayhouse.co.uk

Published in India by: Hay House Publishers India,
Muskaan Complex, Plot No. 3, B-2, Vasant Kunj, New Delhi 110 070
Phone: 91-11-4176-1620 • *Fax:* 91-11-4176-1630
www.hayhouse.co.in

———

**Access New Knowledge.
Anytime. Anywhere.**

Learn and evolve at your own pace
with the world's leading experts.

www.hayhouseU.com